D1294594

Just like me

For my family.
Who always love and accept me for being, well, just like me.

Katie, Ellie and Amelie, you inspired me to write this book!
Keep being your best selves!

- LG

A STUDIO PRESS BOOK

First published in the UK in 2021 by Studio Press,
an imprint of Bonnier Books UK,
The Plaza, 535 King's Road, London SW10 0SZ
Owned by Bonnier Books,
Sveavägen 56, Stockholm, Sweden

www.studiopressbooks.co.uk
www.bonnierbooks.co.uk

Text © 2021 Louise Gooding
Illustration © 2021 Studio Press

3 5 7 9 10 8 6 4 2

All rights reserved
ISBN 978-1-78741-848-6

Edited by Frankie Jones
Illustrated by Angel Chang, Caterina delli Carri, Dante Gabriel Hookey, Melissa Iwai
Designed by Nia Williams
Production by Emma Kidd

The stories in the book follow forty individuals living with various illnesses and disabilities: neurological, physical and learning. Not everyone who lives with one of the illnesses or disabilities featured will have the same symptoms, treatments or journey as those featured in this book. Disabilities and illnesses manifest themselves differently, presenting unique challenges and experiences and having various degrees of impact on a person's life. The summaries of each of the illnesses and disabilities featured are significantly simplified so to give the reader an introduction to the conditions. Further reading on any of the illnesses and disabilities, and people, featured in this book is highly recommended.

The views in this book are the author's own and the copyright, trademarks and names are that of their respective owners and are not intended to suggest endorsement, agreement, affiliation or otherwise of any kind.

A CIP catalogue for this book is available from the British Library
Printed and bound in Latvia

40 neurologically and physically diverse
people who broke stereotypes

Just like me

LOUISE GOODING

STUDIO
PRESS

CONTENTS

iNTRODUCTiON

The world is full of people who are a little different, in one way or another.

Our uniqueness is what makes us who we are.

You may wear glasses, you may have freckles, have albinism, no hair, red hair... even blue hair!

Maybe you are the tallest or the shortest in your family, the loudest or the quietest, the slowest or the fastest. Some differences are easily seen, some may be hidden, but even when it comes down to our fingerprints, we are all unique.

In this book, we follow the stories of forty amazing individuals from all four corners of the globe who have challenged the misconceptions of living with an illness, disability or mental health issue, and shown the world what they can do.

People who have, despite being told they couldn't, shouldn't or even that it was not possible, changed other people's opinions and ideas of what was or wasn't possible for someone living with a disability or difference.

People with dreams who knew, with a bit of determination and perseverance, they could find a way to reach their goals.

Naoki Higashida wanted to be heard, even though he could not speak.

Harriet Tubman wanted freedom, in a country that had enslaved her.

Nkosi Johnson wanted to be loved, in a world in which he was feared.

Dreams come in all shapes and sizes.

Maybe your dream is to learn how to shoot an arrow as far as Matt Stutzman can, to be an artist like Frida Kahlo, to speak in public without a stutter like King George VI did, or maybe to become a world-famous astrophysicist like Stephen Hawking!

Some of the world's most inspirational scientists, artists, engineers, actors, singers, athletes and writers have been people who have had to find a way to overcome their own challenges and differences. People who, until now, you may not have heard of, or who may not of yet had the chance to share their stories.

When I started to write this book, I wrote it with my three children in mind. One was diagnosed as having mild Asperger's, one with ADHD and the other had suffered from discitis when she was only two years old, resulting in years of chronic back pain, physiotherapy and medication. I wanted to find role models, people who my children could learn from and feel inspired by. How do people, like my girls, overcome the potential limitations of their diagnosis and show the world a label need not define who they were or who they would become?

We are all special.
We are all unique.
We are all 'different; not less'.

– Louise Gooding

♪ LUDWIG VAN BEETHOVEN ♪

1770 - 1827

"It seemed unthinkable for me to leave the world forever before I had produced all that I felt called upon to produce."

Ludwig Van Beethoven was born in Bonn, Germany in December 1770.

Ludwig's father had high hopes for his son's musical abilities, pushing him to become a musical prodigy. With daily practice on his piano and violin, and additional lessons on the organ, music was drummed into him. At the age of seven, Ludwig held his first public performance.

Although Ludwig didn't quite become a child star like his father had hoped, he did enjoy improvisation: making up his own music. He later started to gain attention for his musicality, composing his first piece of music at the age of twelve!

In his twenties, Ludwig set off for Vienna, Austria, the home of another world-famous composer: Wolfgang Amadeus Mozart, to study music.

Ludwig was dedicated to improving his performance skills and continuing his studies. With the opportunity to be trained by many highly skilled teachers in violin, vocal composition and musical theory, he was destined for great things. To fund his studies, Ludwig would often play the piano for the rich and famous of Vienna.

As an extremely talented musician, Ludwig had no time for people who didn't pay full attention to his performances. Ludwig was known to stop playing mid-performance and wait for people to stop chatting and focus their attention back on him, before he continued to play.

Ludwig's journey to become a great composer was not without its challenges. By his late twenties, he developed a loud ringing noise in his ears, known as tinnitus. Because of this, he found himself to be hearing-impaired.

The loss of hearing brought great sadness to Ludwig; music was his life and it was meant to be listened to and enjoyed. It was this passion for music that encouraged him to work through his hearing impairment and continue doing what he loved best for as long as he could.

When Ludwig released his first symphony, performed in a famous concert hall in Vienna, it was considered a joke. His experimental style took symphonies to a place where no symphony had been before, breaking the rules and setting a new path for classical music.

ACHIEVEMENTS

Ludwig went on to become one of the world's most famous composers. He wrote some of the most beautiful classical pieces of music ever written: piano concertos, string quartets, piano sonatas and even an opera which took him approximately ten years to perfect. His most recognised piece is *Symphony No. 5* with its strong, dramatic leading four notes.

Although his hearing loss made playing concerts difficult, Ludwig continued to compose, conduct and perform even after he completely lost his hearing. He wouldn't let a single thing, not even going completely deaf, get in the way of his success.

Ludwig's real date of birth is unknown, although records show he was baptised on December 17th. At this time it was the law for babies to be baptised within twenty-four hours of their birth, but there is no proof of his actual date of birth.

What is deafness?

Deafness and hearing loss occur when a person's ability to hear sound is not as clear as it should be, due to inner ear problems or nerve damage.

Hearing loss or partial deafness limits a person's ability to correctly hear sounds. Today, hearing aids, which are special devices worn inside the ear, can help project sounds.

Those who are profoundly deaf have a total loss of sound, relying on lip reading and sign language as a way to communicate with others. Some people can still feel sound through vibrations and many deaf people are still able to watch and enjoy movies and television with the help of subtitles and signing.

"I understand and appreciate the air we breathe a little more than most."

Jerome Bettis was born in Michigan, USA on February 16th, 1972.

Growing up in a rough area of Detroit, Jerome's parents were determined to keep him and his siblings off the streets and out of trouble. Most of Jerome's time was spent with his family. His mother was a bowling instructor and was keen to encourage her children to be involved with the sport.

In his spare time, Jerome enjoyed playing street football with the other kids. With his small frame and being asthmatic, Jerome wasn't picked first to join any of the teams, nor did the kids see him as much of a threat on the field. This never deterred Jerome from playing, and at the age of twelve he found himself growing taller, bigger and stronger than all the other boys. No one wanted to challenge him now!

Wanting to follow in his father's footsteps, Jerome had plans to become an electrical engineer. But, as the family didn't have much money, the only way he would get the chance to study at college would be if he found himself a sports scholarship.

Jerome was talented in both bowling and American football, but no colleges were offering a fully-funded scholarship for bowling. This made the decision easier for Jerome. He chose American football.

Jerome was built for American football. He was big and strong and was soon nicknamed 'The

Bus', due to his ability to keep pushing forward, despite tacklers from the opposing team clinging onto him. He made it look like he was giving them a ride down the field.

Jerome had been diagnosed with asthma as a teenager and this was something he needed to keep in mind, considering the amount of sport he played and the fitness that was required. After suffering a serious asthma attack in a game, needing immediate medical assistance, Jerome made sure to always keep his asthma in check. By making regular appointments with his doctors and monitoring his condition, they could keep his asthma under control with medication when required. By doing this he continued to have a successful and long career within American football.

ACHIEVEMENTS
Jerome's career in American football had only just begun when he received his scholarship, playing football for Notre Dame College. He was later drafted to The Rams, a professional American football team based in Los Angeles where he played for two years before moving to the Pittsburgh Steelers, where he played for a further nine years until his retirement.

He won a number of awards in his career in American football, including a Lifetime Achievement Award for his effort and commitment to the Pittsburgh Steelers.

In 2006, Jerome was given an honorary doctoral degree from Lawrence Technological University, Michigan.

Jerome founded the 'The Bus Stops Here Foundation' to help improve the lives of underprivileged inner city kids and schools. His work with the foundation supplied both academic and sporting grants to help give more children the chance to get into further education.

What is asthma?

Asthma is a long-term condition that affects the lungs, causing the airways to narrow and/or swell, leaving the person feeling short of breath and unable to get enough oxygen to the brain. There are many different types and causes of asthma, with symptoms and attacks ranging from mild to severe.

Someone having an asthma attack may feel tightness in the chest, feel unable to breathe, and may cough and wheeze.

People with asthma can control their symptoms by using inhalers and medicines to help keep their airways open. It is important to be aware of what may trigger asthma; things such as exercise, pollen, pet hair, dust, cold air and perfumes can cause asthma attacks.

"I take things one step at a time."

Simone Biles was born in Ohio, USA on March 14th, 1997.

Simone was raised by her grandfather from the age of three. Simone's mother was unfortunately unable to provide a safe and stable home life for Simone and her siblings. Luckily for Simone, her grandfather and his wife adopted her and her sister.

At the age of six, Simone went on a field trip to watch some local gymnasts in training. Simone was blown away. Standing on the sidelines with her group, Simone found herself mimicking their movements and poses. Some of the coaches had noticed her and made sure to give Simone an enrolment form, encouraging her to join the club. Simone did just that.

Whilst Simone was smaller than the rest of the girls, it didn't mean she was weaker. Instead, Simone pushed herself harder. If someone told her she couldn't do a trick, she worked her hardest until she had mastered it. She was so determined to succeed as a gymnast that her grandparents started to home school her, allowing Simone to dedicate more of her free time to gymnastics. She put thirty-two hours a week into training! Simone had a lot of energy and was diagnosed with having ADHD as a young girl. She had been regularly taking medicine to help manage her symptoms, but because her ADHD did not define who she was, Simone and her family chose not to publicly discuss it.

An opportunity came up for Simone to try out for a place on Team USA for the 2016 Rio

Olympics. All those years of hard work paid off. She was given a place on the team and was going to Rio!

Simone was busy preparing for the games when some unpleasant people appeared online, determined to sabotage her place on the team. They had stolen her private medical records and claimed that as she was on medication, she should be disqualified. The medication was called Ritalin, the medication she had been using to help manage her ADHD. Simone came forward and told the world about her ADHD. She was not ashamed, or embarrassed to say she had ADHD, it was part of who she was. She would not be made to feel bad for taking medication she knew helped control her symptoms. The accusations were dismissed, her place on the team was safe.

ACHIEVEMENTS

Simone has so far won over 30 World Championship and Olympic medals. She has also won many awards around the world for her sporting achievements and was named one of the most influential people in the world by *Time* magazine in 2017.

Having won so many awards and medals in her early gymnastics career, it was of no surprise that Simone won four gold medals at the Rio Olympics. She has been acknowledged as the best and most decorated female gymnast in history, and in the media, as the world's greatest female gymnast.

Simone is an advocate for foster kids. After discovering that only about three percent of foster kids went on to gain a bachelor's degree, compared to thirty percent of the general population, she launched a scholarship fund to help assist foster children with costs towards gaining a degree. Simone believes that everybody, no matter their background, deserves the chance and opportunity to learn.

What is ADHD?

ADHD stands for Attention Deficit Hyperactivity Disorder and is something that is usually diagnosed in childhood. ADHD can last into adulthood.

It is not clear what causes ADHD, but it seems to be hereditary, meaning it tends to run in families. ADHD affects 'executive functions' in the brain, the part that controls concentration, self-control and organisational skills. There are many different options for treatment including medication, behavioural therapy, parental coaching and support through school.

There are three types of ADHD: attentive, inattentive and combined. ADHD is likely be diagnosed alongside other disorders, such as anxiety, autism spectrum, ODD, bipolar, sleep disorder and learning disabilities.

*"I have shown that anything is possible.
I always tell people not to limit themselves."*

Usain Bolt was born in Montego Bay, Jamaica on August 21st, 1986.

As a young boy, Usain would often be found on the streets playing cricket with his younger brother. Using an orange as a ball and banana tree stumps for the wicket, they would keep themselves busy whilst their parents ran the family grocery store.

Usain had a keen interest in sports, and when he entered high school, he showed promise as a fast bowler in cricket. However, it was Usain's cricket coach at school who noticed his phenomenal speed whilst watching Usain run up to bowl. With the encouragement of his cricket coach, Usain began training in track and field athletics. The head of sports at his school, seeing Usain's talent, gifted Usain his first pair of track shoes. This aided Usain's technique on the track and helped keep him motivated. Usain soon discovered he was the fastest runner in his school.

By the time he was fifteen, Usain took part in the World Junior Championships, which was being held in Kingston, Jamaica. He won gold in the 200 metre sprint, becoming the youngest athlete to win a gold medal in the games. He also took home two silver medals: for the 100 metre sprint and as part of a team in the 400 metre relay. He was on his way to achieving great things!

Training didn't always come so easy for Usain. When he was younger, he had been diagnosed with something called scoliosis, an abnormal curvature in his spine. His scoliosis would occasionally limit his progress due to pain. Usain did not know much about his condition but, to help ease some of his discomfort, his coach put together a special programme to help Usain strengthen his core and back muscles; providing extra support and stability for his spine, which in turn eased some of the pain.

With a lot of hard work and a strong competitive streak, Usain wanted to prove he was not just a great athlete, but could be the greatest!

ACHIEVEMENTS

Usain competed in the Olympics, the World Championships, Diamond League and Commonwealth Games, winning medal after medal and smashing world records. He earned the nickname 'Lightning Bolt' and was often seen striking a lightning bolt pose before and after his races.

Usain has claimed nineteen world records including the fastest 100 metre, fastest 150 metre, fastest 200 metre, the most medals won and many more. He has nine Olympic gold medals, has won numerous awards for his sporting achievements, and is one of the highest paid athletes in the world.

Usain considered a career in football after he retired from track and field in 2017. He played for a team in Norway for a short while and also for a team in Australia before announcing in 2019 that he was going to retire from all sport.

What is scoliosis?

Scoliosis is an abnormal curvature of the spine. The curvature develops in an S or C shape. Although you can be born with scoliosis, it often develops during childhood.

Scoliosis is more common in women and tends to run in families. Sometimes, scoliosis can develop when there is an abnormality elsewhere in the body, like one leg being longer than the other. The spine then creates an artificial curve to correct the balance.

Scoliosis can cause pain or tiredness following long stretches of standing or sitting. Treatment varies from person to person, depending on the degree of curvature in their spine; core muscle training and strengthening, back braces, physiotherapy, pain medication and, in some cases, surgery may be needed.

"My general attitude to life is to enjoy every minute of every day."

Richard Branson was born in London, England on July 18th, 1950.

When Richard was a toddler his mother noticed he seemed a little different from other children his age. He struggled with his coordination, and it was also sometimes very difficult to understand what he was trying to say. When learning his letters and numbers, he didn't seem to understand their meaning, or why the sounds should match the symbol that was being shown to him.

Richard was diagnosed as having dyslexia. His mother understood that dyslexia may make a lot of things more difficult for Richard to master. She set about creating challenges to build his confidence and encourage him to keep going.

At school Richard got on well with others. He was the captain of many of the school's sports teams and was often praised for his athletic abilities. In the classroom however, Richard struggled. He couldn't keep up with the other students and was moved to a boarding school in the hope they could provide more support for his dyslexia.

Richard still struggled, his teachers allowed no excuses, not even for his dyslexia. Richard had to move schools again, where he continued to battle with reading and writing, due to the lack of support for children with dyslexia.

Richard was sixteen when he decided to leave school and move back to London. He set up a magazine called *Student*, which was published by students, for students. Richard had so many companies wanting to pay for advertising in his magazine that he was able to print and distribute the magazine for free.

The magazine was doing well when Richard had his second business idea: a mail order record company which he named Virgin Records. He soon had enough money to open a store that sold discounted music and records. Another two years went by and Richard was yet again ready to try something new. Using the money he had earned from his store, he formed a record label which would allow him to now produce and promote music, not just sell it. Some of the biggest names in music were signed to his record label.

ACHIEVEMENTS

Richard's adventures as an entrepreneur didn't end with the creation of the Virgin record label. He was able to see opportunities to develop his ideas and was brave enough to take risks to see where they led him.

He is now known as one of the wealthiest and most successful people in the world, winning many awards for his businesses and breaking world records along the way!

Alongside running his businesses, which now includes an airline and travel company, Richard makes time to support many different charities, helping people who have suffered from natural or man-made disasters.

Richard dreams of being the first business to offer commercial space travel, and launched Virgin Galactic in 2004. With tickets for a ninety-minute flight costing hundreds of thousands of pounds, it looks as though, for now, being able to see Earth from the edge of space won't be accessible or affordable for all.

What is dyslexia?

Dyslexia is a learning disability that affects the ability of someone to read, write and sometimes speak. Just because a person has dyslexia, it doesn't mean they aren't clever. Dyslexia is usually hereditary, meaning it can run in the family.

Dyslexia equally affects boys and girls but it is normally easier and quicker to spot the signs of dyslexia in boys. There is no cure for dyslexia but treatments are available in the form of structured programmes, therapy and other tools to help with reading.

RALPH BRAUN

1940 - 2013

"Rise above my friends, and reach back and help others climb the ladder of life."

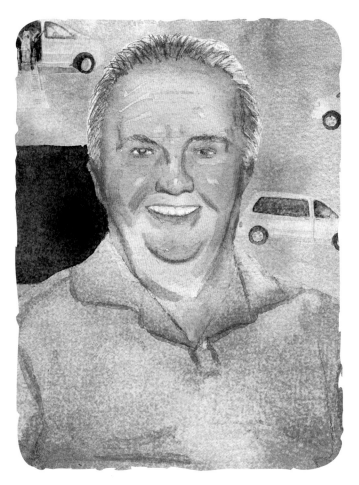

Ralph Braun was born in Indiana, USA on December 18th, 1940.

As a young boy, Ralph couldn't easily keep up with his friends and family, even climbing the stairs after his siblings proved a challenge.

His parents realised that something wasn't quite right and took him to the doctor to get some answers. After many tests, at the age of six, Ralph was diagnosed with having muscular dystrophy. Ralph's parents were told that he would probably never live past his teens. They were even asked if they would consider leaving Ralph at the hospital, so the doctors could study the progression of his condition, something his parents were appalled to be asked!

As Ralph grew older, his condition got worse and he soon became dependent on using a wheelchair. When Ralph was growing up, things weren't as accessible as they are today. Ramps were not readily available, meaning that people in wheelchairs were not always able to live independently and/or access a number of places or use public transport.

Ralph later dropped out of high school, fed up with the daily battle to get around the campus in his wheelchair. He realised, after being re-diagnosed with spinal muscular atrophy, a condition that would not have such a devastating impact on his life expectancy, that he would need to find a way to gain his independence.

At fifteen, Ralph set about inventing a motorised wheelchair, designing and welding it himself. He had often watched his cousins and uncles in their garage, tinkering with engines. Ralph was a natural, and although his first prototype was far too big and bulky to easily use at home, it gave Ralph the idea to create a three-wheeled scooter.

Ralph started working at a local factory as a quality control technician. Getting to and from work was still a bit of a challenge on his scooter. Not one to give up, Ralph bought himself an old postal van and decided he was going to make some adjustments so that he could drive this to work. He designed a lift that would raise him and his scooter into the back of the van. Ralph's talent for engineering once again helped him keep his independence.

ACHIEVEMENTS

Word soon spread about Ralph's three-wheeled scooter and his vehicle lift, and he started getting enquiries asking if he would help make them for others. Soon Ralph was able to give up his job at the factory and started up his own company, The Braun Corporation, which went on to become a worldwide business specialising in wheelchair-accessible vehicles, lifts and mobility.

He was awarded The Champion of Change Honour by the White House in 2012, for his dedication to helping people with physical disabilities and leading education and employment efforts in science, technology, engineering and maths for Americans with disabilities.

Ralph set up a non-profit company called NOVA: National Organisation for Vehicle Accessibility, to help bridge the funding gap for those who could not afford the adaptions to their transport, or mobility products. NOVA has since moved on to offer a greater range of services to people needing access to mobility products and support.

What is spinal muscular atrophy?

Spinal muscular atrophy is a motor neurone disease; the damaged nerve cells (or motor neurones) in the brain and spinal cord affect the nervous system, leaving it unable to send messages to the muscles responsible for movement. The muscles most affected by this genetic disease are the ones closest to the core of the body: the thighs, shoulders and hips. There are different types of spinal muscular atrophy which have different affects, depending on the age of onset or the severity of the disease. Treatment is available in the form on physical therapy, nutrition and medication. There is no cure as yet for spinal muscular atrophy.

CHANTELLE BROWN-YOUNG

*"I have my flaws, but I love them,
I embrace them, they're mine."*

Chantelle Brown-Young was born in Toronto, Canada, on July 27th, 1994.

Chantelle was raised alongside her siblings by her single mother in Toronto. At the age of four Chantelle's family noticed that she had some light spots appearing on her skin, her knees, her neck and above her eyes. A doctor diagnosed Chantelle with having vitiligo.

At first Chantelle didn't notice her skin, it was just how her skin was. But when Chantelle started to go to school, the other children started to pick on her, making nasty comments about her skin, calling her names and making her feel very self-conscious.

Chantelle moved schools again and again, but the bullying continued. At one school she started to make friends, then the next day at school the children refused to go near her. Unsure of what she had done, she asked. One girl's parents had told their daughter to stay away from Chantelle in case they caught her vitiligo. Of course this wasn't possible, but no one thought to ask.

Chantelle grew up to be a tall and beautiful young lady, who still felt self-conscious about her skin. A journalist came across her on Instagram and asked to interview her about her vitiligo. After the interview, the journalist suggested Chantelle consider a career in modelling.

'Why not?' thought Chantelle. Maybe her difference could be an asset and set her apart from everyone else, but every modelling agency she contacted turned her down. Undeterred Chantelle decided to take the matter into her own hands and embrace her individuality. She was going to be a model, and Winnie Harlow was born.

Winnie Harlow, Chantelle's alter ego, was fierce and would let nothing stand in her way. She was determined to put in all the hard work needed to make it in the modelling industry. She was soon spotted by the producers of a reality television show, where a group of potential models were put against each other on the runway, in photoshoots and various challenges to battle for the top spot and the chance to be crowned 'America's Next Top Model'.

ACHIEVEMENTS

Chantelle didn't win *America's Next Top Model*, but she has gone on to become one of the world's most recognised models. Chantelle has walked some of the most iconic runways, been photographed by some of the most renowned photographers and appeared in campaigns internationally. She has been on the cover of some of the most famous fashion magazines around the world. She has also worked with different international charity groups to raise money for people in need and helped support the company Burts Bees with their #bringbackthebees campaign, to spread awareness of the importance of bees in our ecosystem.

Chantelle did a TEDxTeen Talk about what beauty means, talking about her own journey and how growing up with vitiligo led to being bullied. Chantelle wants others to look at how beauty is defined, and not let it be determined by other people's opinions or what we see, read or hear in the media.

What is vitiligo?

It's not actually known what causes vitiligo, but it is assumed to be an autoimmune disorder. The body's immune system attacks its own healthy cells, tissues and organs. With vitiligo, the immune system attacks the cells in the skin: those that are responsible for protecting the skin from UV rays and that determine the colour of our skin, known as melanin. This causes white patches to appear on the skin or hair of the person affected. You cannot catch vitiligo, and it affects all ages, genders and all ethnic groups equally.

SUDHA CHANDRAN

"I take inspiration from my failures. When people tell me, 'you can't do this', or 'you're not eligible to do this', or 'it is not meant for you', these things incite me to prove myself."

Sudha Chandran was born in Mumbai, India on September 27th, 1965.

Everything was about dance to young Sudha. She started her dancing lessons at the age of three and a half, studying Bharatanatyam, a form of South Indian Dance and she adored everything about it.

Sudha's parents, seeing her love of dance, took her to audition at a famous dance school near to where they lived. The school wasn't interested, as Sudha was far too young. Her parents begged the school to watch their daughter dance before they returned home. After agreeing, the school principle was absolutely spellbound watching Sudha dance. The school decided to make an exception and she was enrolled straight away.

By sixteen Sudha had performed in front of hundreds of people. Her future in dance looked promising.

Then disaster struck. Sudha had been making her way home from a pilgrimage with her parents when the bus they were travelling on was involved in a traffic accident. Many passengers were hurt, including Sudha, whose legs got stuck in the wreckage.

Sudha had to be treated for a broken bone and a few small cuts, but as there were many other people with more severe injuries, the doctors were quick to send her home. Unfortunately, in their rush the doctors had missed a cut on Sudha's foot, which soon became infected. By the time Sudha returned to the hospital the infection had spread and had turned into gangrene.

The only thing the doctors could do now was to amputate her right leg, just below the knee, to stop the infection from spreading, or worse, killing her.

After the amputation Sudha was given a Jaipur leg, a rubber-based prosthetic, used widely in India by people with a below-the-knee amputation. She would have to learn to walk all over again. It took Sudha three years to recover from the accident. Determined not to let her accident put a stop to her dancing dreams, she returned to her training. It was going to be a difficult journey but Sudha knew she had to do it and believed that if she put her mind to it, anything was possible!

ACHIEVEMENTS

Sudha's first public performance gained a lot of media attention. Word had spread about the accident and how hard she had worked on her return to dance. The show sold out and was met with a standing ovation at the end of her performance.

Sudha was asked if she would be interested in making a film about her life with the opportunity to play herself in the lead role. The film, *Telugu*, was extremely successful and led the way for Sudha to start a career in Bollywood. Sudha has starred in many movies and in many television series. She is one of the most famous Bollywood actresses in India.

As a chairperson for The National Association of Disabilities Enterprises (NADE), based in Mumbai, Sudha helps disabled people in India find employment and access equal opportunities. Around 120 million people in India identify with being disabled. NADE aims to educate businesses about the employment of disabled people and motivate disabled persons to seek work if they feel capable.

What is gangrene?

Gangrene occurs when body tissue dies. There are many different types of gangrene, and many different causes including infection, restricted/loss of blood flow, illness or injury. Usually gangrene affects toes, fingers and the limbs, but it can also have an affect inside the body.

Gangrene is treatable with the removal of the dead tissue and with the help of antibiotics. If gangrene found on the digits or limbs is not immediately treated, amputation may be the only option to help stop the spread of the infection. Gangrene is a very serious condition that needs immediate medical attention as it can be fatal.

CONNIE CHIU

"Appreciate people who help you, and surround yourself with good people who see and love you for the person you are, for all that you are."

Connie Chiu was born in Kowloon, Hong Kong, in 1969.

Growing up in the city of Kowloon, Connie noticed she looked a little different to everyone else around her. She had been born with albinism, a condition that gave her very pale skin, blue eyes and bright white hair. No one around her, not even in her own family, had this condition. She often wondered if there were other people that looked like she did. She surely couldn't be the only person in the world living with albinism.

In Kowloon, the sun can be very intense and Connie needed to wear sunglasses to protect her eyes and carry a parasol to protect her sensitive skin. She often found herself getting burnt, so had to take extra precautions to protect herself. Connie's parents decided it would be better to move away from Kowloon and go somewhere Connie would not have to worry so much about the sun's effect on her skin. The family packed up all their belongings and moved to Sweden.

The move was great for Connie. Her new school promoted acceptance and equality. She never felt singled out or bullied because of her difference, and, in her first year living in Sweden, Connie won a beauty competition.

At the age of twenty-one, Connie was asked to model for an end-of-year fashion show for her sister. A born performer, Connie loved all the excitement of being backstage and being surrounded by so many beautiful clothes. She loved it so much that she was inspired to send some head shots to a very famous fashion designer to see if she could get the chance to walk the runway again.

Four months later, Connie received a phone call asking if she would represent the designer in a fashion show in Paris. Of course Connie said yes! After her first big show she continued to work hard, contacting different designers, directors and photographers who were all impressed with Connie's drive, attitude, looks and determination. Connie's career in modelling had begun!

ACHIEVEMENTS

Connie became the first professional model with albinism, and in doing so, inspired others with albinism to follow their dreams. She credits her success on growing up in an environment that allowed her to be herself. She was able to feel happy, confident and embrace who she was, never fearing judgement from others.

Her albinism allowed her to stand out and because people took notice of her, she used this as a platform to raise awareness of albinism around the world. She wanted to be the role model that she never had.

Connie first performed as a jazz musician in 2011 and has since performed regularly at various festivals, clubs and events around the world. Not only does she sing, but she plays guitar and writes her own compositions. She released a debut album in 2015 called *Huckleberry Songs*.

What is albinism?

Albinism is a genetic condition, present from birth. Approximately one in twenty thousand people are born with albinism. A lack of pigmentation affects the colour of a person's skin, hair and eyes. The lack of pigmentation, or melanin, means that the person is more sensitive to sun exposure and is more prone to sunburn.

It is quite common for someone born with albinism to also have vision problems due to an under development in the central part of the eye that is responsible for sharp, detailed vision. This may also make them sensitive to light.

BRAD COHEN

"Everyone, regardless of ability or disability, has strengths and weaknesses. Know what yours are and build on your strengths and find a way around your weaknesses."

Brad Cohen was born in the USA, on December 18th, 1973.

Brad was not born with Tourette's, but it was something that developed in his early childhood. From about seven years of age he would twitch and randomly make loud noises throughout the day. Brad didn't mean to do these things, he couldn't control the tics the Tourette's gave him. Brad wasn't diagnosed with Tourette's until the age of twelve which made it hard for others to understand his behaviour. Brad's father found it excruciatingly difficult to deal with and would often berate Brad for making barking noises and for his constant fidgeting.

Teachers at school assumed Brad was just a disruptive child. One teacher even called Brad up to the front of the class, forcing him to apologise for his behaviour. His classmates would often call him names and make fun of him.

Once Brad was finally given his diagnosis, his mother found a local support group, thinking it would help Brad to meet others like him, to know he wasn't alone. They walked in and found a group of people who seemed very depressed and defeated by their Tourette's. Brad was shocked, he took the decision there and then, that he was never going to let Tourette's beat him, he was going to work his hardest to find a way to succeed.

Brad had decided when he was quite young that he wanted to train as a teacher when he grew up. There was a need for diversity in education and a better understanding of kids living with differences and Brad wanted to help start that change.

Brad graduated from college with top marks and had a lot of glowing recommendations under his belt from his various school placements. It was now time to find himself a job. He applied to over twenty teaching positions in different schools, but each school turned him down, concerned his Tourette's would affect his teaching abilities.

Feeling deflated, but determined not to give up, Brad kept applying to schools in Georgia until at last one school, who believed in celebrating diversity, decided to give Brad a chance.

Brad finally got to show everyone how great a teacher he could be.

ACHIEVEMENTS

Brad became an extraordinary teacher! By the end of his first year of teaching, Brad was the recipient of the State of Georgia's First Class Teacher of the Year award! At the start of his placement, some parents had been unsure how someone with Tourette's could possibly take charge of a class. Some parents even requested to have their child taken out of the class, but after winning his award, parents were all desperate for their child to be taught by Brad. Brad set up a foundation, under his own name, that helps children living with Tourette's realise their potential, challenge perceptions and follow their dreams.

Brad wrote about his life in an autobiography, *Front of the Class: How Tourette Syndrome Made Me the Teacher I Never Had*. The book was later turned into a film under the same name. The actors who played Brad in his childhood and as a young man had to do intense training to understand how to play someone with Tourette's, having never lived with the condition themselves.

What is Tourette's?

Tourette's is a neurological condition that causes a person to make repetitive, involuntary movements and sounds called tics. The onset of tics has been likened to the feeling or need that you are going to sneeze. Common tics are coughing, sniffing, barking, blinking and head jerking. Tics are often made worse by overexcitement or stress.

Most cases of Tourette's appear between the ages of five and ten, affecting a higher number of boys than girls. Tourette's may improve with age or disappear completely. Treatment is available in the form of behavioural therapy and, occasionally, medication.

KADEENA COX

*"MS is not the end of your life.
it doesn't put a full stop after your name."*

Kadeena Cox was born in Leeds, England on March 10th, 1991.

Kadeena was very active and sporty when she was young. Whilst training, her hockey coach spotted how quick she was on her feet and encouraged her to give track sprinting a try.

She certainly was a strong and talented sprinter. By the age of fifteen she was competing in regional tournaments and won a bronze medal at the Manchester Open: under-17 category. Kadeena looked set to having a promising career as a potential Olympic sprinter, as she was able to run one hundred metres in under twelve seconds.

Kadeena was keen to also pursue her education alongside her sporting dreams and went to university to study physiotherapy. At twenty-three years old, and partially through her studies, Kadeena had a stroke, and within the next few months was diagnosed with having Multiple Sclerosis. Kadeena had noticed a tingling in her arm that spread through her limbs, it was painful and made the right side of her body weaker than the left.

Kadeena was warned this may be the end of her career as a runner, and that she would need to undergo a lot of physiotherapy to build her strength up again. She was determined to find a way to get herself back into training and sports. Taking a year out of university, she concentrated hard with the help of her rehabilitation physiotherapist to reach her goals. She wanted to take this time to do something special, whilst many were telling her that she couldn't, or shouldn't,

Kadeena was determined to get herself back to competitive sports.

Training was hard, she needed to work on her coordination and balance, as the stroke had left her slightly unstable. Finding herself too wobbly to use weights, she sat herself down on a stationary bike. All those years of running had giving her strong legs, perfect for cycling. Someone noticed her natural talent and suggested she contact British Cycling.

With a lot of hard work, determination and passion, Kadeena achieved her goal to return to sports. Not only that, she had worked so hard that she was awarded a place on the Great British Paralympic team, as both a track athlete and as a para-cyclist.

ACHIEVEMENTS
Kadeena was the second person in English history to win gold medals in two different sports in the Paralympic Games when she took part in the 2016 games in Rio. She finished with a gold, silver and bronze for her sprint races and a gold in para-cycling. Kadeena has also won many medals by competing in the World Para Athletics European and World Championships and the Union Cycliste Internationale Para-cycling Track World Championships. In 2017, having represented her country so successfully, she was honoured with an MBE by the Queen of England for her services to athletics.

Kadeena finally got her degree, graduating from Manchester University in July 2019.

Kadeena loves reality television shows and has appeared in many herself, from whipping up tasty treats in *The Great British Bake Off* to raise money for Stand Up To Cancer, to testing her brain power in *Mastermind*, where her specialist subject was Arsenal Football Club. She even co-created a robot, which won all four of its rounds in a celebrity edition of *Robot Wars*.

What is Multiple Sclerosis?

Multiple Sclerosis, otherwise known as MS, is an autoimmune disease that affects the central nervous system: the brain, the spinal cord and nerves. The immune system attacks myelin, a fatty material that is wrapped around the nerve fibres to protect them. This leaves scars which prevents the brain from being able to send or receive signals as it should. Multiple Sclerosis is a lifelong condition but can be treated with medication and therapy.

Each person diagnosed with MS is unique. There isn't just one specific cause of the disease, so every person's symptoms and treatments will be different.

"Even though someone has dwarfism, they are the exact same on the inside – with hopes and dreams and fears – they are exactly the same but in a slightly different shaped body."

Warwick Davis was born in Surrey, England on February 3rd, 1970.

When Warwick was born, the doctor asked his father to stand up, looked him up and down, declared he wasn't unusually short, and left the room. Warwick was born with Spondyloepiphyseal Dysplasia Congenita, a very rare form of dwarfism. This meant he would never grow as tall as the average person. His parents were told that his case was so severe, that they didn't expect Warwick to live past his teenage years.

Warwick attended school like everyone else. Worried that Warwick's short stature would lead the other children to pick on him at school, his father encouraged Warwick to develop a good sense of humour and be confident. Warwick's father didn't want anyone to feel they could bully him, and Warwick made sure he held his head high.

When Warwick was eleven years old, his grandmother heard an advert on the radio, asking for people under four feet tall to audition for a *Star Wars* movie. Warwick, being a huge *Star Wars* fan, was delighted to be given the opportunity to appear in one of his favourite movies, so he auditioned for a role.

Warwick was cast as an extra, but after one of the lead actors became ill, Warwick found himself playing the part of the lead Ewok.

The producer of *Star Wars*, George Lucas, was so impressed with Warwick's natural talent that he contacted him about a new project he was working on. *Willow* was written with Warwick in mind. The film was about a young apprentice magician who, with the help of a great swordsman, journeyed through a land filled with magic and monsters in order to save a baby princess from an evil queen.

The film was a success and Warwick has gone on to star in many other films and television shows throughout his career: playing characters from wizards, to leprechauns, goblins and even appearing just as himself.

ACHIEVEMENTS

With his strong, vibrant personality and good sense of humour, Warwick wants to show people living with dwarfism that, although things can be tough at times, there is a lot you can achieve and a lot of joy to be found when you embrace who you are.

Warwick lives with his wife and their two children in England. He met his wife, who also has a form of dwarfism, achondroplasia, on the set of *Willow*. Their two children, who have inherited Warwick's dwarfism, have followed in their parents' footsteps and are also actors.

In 2011 Warwick wrote an autobiography about his life called *Size Matters Not*.

Warwick not only acts, but he also runs his own talent agency called Willow Management. The agency supports and represents actors under five feet tall, or those who are over seven feet tall. He is also the co-founder of Little People UK, a charity that supports families and people living with dwarfism.

What is Spondyloepiphyseal Dysplasia Congenita?

Spondyloepiphyseal Dysplasia Congenita, often shortened to SED or SDC, is a genetic bone growth disorder that results in this very rare form of dwarfism.

It is caused by a mutation in the gene that controls a special protein that the body uses to make bones and cartilage. People with SED only grow to between three to four feet in height. Their hands and feet are of average size but their bodies, arms and legs are much shorter and their spines may have an abnormal curvature. SED doesn't reduce life expectancy, unless there are any other medical complications.

AARON FOTHERINGHAM

"It's pretty sweet to be able to help people look at their wheelchair as something besides just a medical device and it can actually be something really fun."

Aaron Fotheringham was born in Nevada, USA on November 8th, 1991.

Aaron was born with Spina Bifida and, at two months old, was adopted by Steve and Kayleen Fotheringham.

Growing up, Aaron would need the aid of splints, crutches and a wheelchair to help him to move around. At the age of eight, Aaron decided to use his wheelchair full-time.

Aaron would often go to the skatepark with his dad and older brother, to watch his brother practise tricks and various stunts on his skateboard. Aaron longed to join in, and his brother saw no reason why he couldn't; he already had his own set of wheels, so why not give it a try?

Together his father and brother helped Aaron get to the top of the ramp in his wheelchair. His first attempt to tackle the ramp didn't go so well, but Aaron just got back up and tried again. He was determined to get the hang of it. With time, patience, practise and a lot of bumps and bruises, he got it!

Aaron soon had a specially designed wheelchair made for him, with suspension to help cushion his landings. It needed to be light enough for him to pull off all the tricks he wanted to learn. Aaron worked closely with the design team to make sure he could show them what he needed.

With his new wheelchair, Aaron would practise his tricks and jumps into a large foam pit. Once he felt confident in his abilities, he would move to the crash mats, before heading to the ramps to tackle his latest move. He was developing a whole new sport, WCMX: wheelchair motor cross. By fourteen, he could back flip in his wheelchair, by eighteen, he was able to do a double backflip!

Aaron always tries to find the advantages of his condition, often stating that without living his life in a wheelchair, he may have never discovered WCMX. By sharing his passion with others, he has been able to inspire people to see wheelchairs as a tool that can literally send them soaring and propel them forward in life.

ACHIEVEMENTS
Aaron has been nominated for a number of awards for his sporting achievements, including best male athlete with a disability.

With his WCMX skills he now tours the world with an action sports roadshow called *Nitro Circus*. *Nitro Circus* allowed Aaron to continue developing his skills and abilities, trying out new things so he could show the world what he could do. Nicknamed Wheelz, he is often seen launching off 50 foot mega ramps, much to the amazement of the crowds.

Aaron also teaches kids who use wheelchairs how exciting they can be by running WCMX courses.

Aaron co-wrote a children's book about achieving your dreams, encouraging kids to use and listen to their own thoughts and feelings, and embrace who they are, supporting one another and not letting anything stand in their way from becoming the person they were born to be. The book is called *Mike Believe; Wheelz On The Moon*.

What is Spina Bifida?

Spina Bifida is a birth defect where the baby's spinal cord fails to develop properly in the first weeks of pregnancy. It can usually be seen and diagnosed by the 18th-22nd week of the baby's development. Most cases of Spina Bifida are diagnosed before birth, but some very mild cases may never be diagnosed.

A person with Spina Bifida may have limited mobility, need to use braces, crutches or a wheelchair. There is no cure, but treatments, and sometimes surgery, are available. Research is still being carried out to determine the cause of Spina Bifida; doctors assume it may be due to a mix of genetic, nutritional and environmental influences.

SELENA GOMEZ

"You are who are; you're unique and you're rare."

Selena Gomez was born in Texas, USA on July 22nd, 1992.

Selena's career in the entertainment industry began at a very early age. At six years old she successfully auditioned for a part in a children's show called *Barney*. Selena's bubbly personality impressed the producers and she was later taken on to work for the Disney Channel. She was cast as one of the lead roles for a show called *Wizards of Waverly Place*.

Selena became a household name, not only as a TV star, but as a pop singer, too. With music singles, albums and world tours, Selena often performed in front of thousands of people.

Then, without warning, Selena went very quiet, avoiding social media and not promoting any of her new music. Selena had been dealing with poor health for quite some time and was told her declining health was due to something called lupus. She needed to pay closer attention to her health.

Choosing to ignore her doctors, Selena carried on with her busy lifestyle, until she found her body was just too weak, forcing her to stop.

Having chosen to ignore the doctors' warnings, Selena was now being told that her kidneys had suffered a lot of damage and she would need a kidney transplant. It was a life or death situation and a very scary time for Selena.

She would need chemotherapy and strong medication, as well as a potential ten year wait for a suitable donor for a new kidney. A close friend found out about her plight and volunteered to get tested, to see if she could be a match. As luck would have it, she was. Selena's friend offered to donate one of her kidneys to Selena to save her life. To Selena, this was the most amazing gift anyone could and would ever give her.

The operation was a success for both Selena and her friend. Selena was told that after the operation it would be extremely unlikely her lupus would return, but she would need to continue to take better care of herself in future.

ACHIEVEMENTS
Selena is a world-famous actress, television producer and singer. She has sold over seven million albums and over twenty-two million singles.

She was named as one of the 2012 Glamour Award Women of the Year. Not only does Selena collaborate with many top name perfume, make-up and fashion brands, but she also has her own fashion line Dream Out Loud, producing clothing made using eco-friendly materials.

Selena is a UNICEF spokesperson, she helps raise awareness of the importance of providing clean water to those living in Ghana, Africa.

Selena loves dogs. She has adopted many dogs over the years from various shelters. One of her dogs was originally saved and taken to a local animal shelter by her father. The shelter said they would have to put the dog down if a home wasn't found for him within a few weeks. Appalled at hearing this, Selena adopted the dog straight away.

What is lupus?

Lupus is a long-term autoimmune disease. Instead of the body's immune system protecting and fighting off infections, it turns on itself, attacking healthy cells, causing inflammation and permanent damage. Lupus mainly affects the skin, joints and internal organs. Anyone can get lupus, and at any age but it predominantly affects women aged between fifteen and forty-four. There is no cure for lupus and its cause is unclear.

Medication and treatment depends on the type of lupus someone has and the severity of the symptoms. There is a high risk of heart disease, kidney disease and stroke if the symptoms are not closely monitored and treated by a doctor.

TEMPLE GRANDIN

"Different; not less."

Temple Grandin was born in Boston, USA on August 29th, 1947.

Temple was noticeably a little different from other children. She did not speak until the age of four. This would sometimes make Temple very angry, as she could not communicate what she wanted to other people. Her mother, seeing Temple's struggle, was determined to get Temple the help and support she needed. Doctors diagnosed Temple with having autism. Delayed speech is quite a common symptom for children with autism, but when Temple was young, not much was really known about autism and its effect on people. It was just assumed that it was some form of brain damage.

Temple had a lot of people who believed in her and, with the help of speech therapy, she learnt to say her first words. Now that Temple had the ability to communicate, she was able to go to a regular preschool. Fitting in at school proved somewhat difficult for Temple as she didn't like to be touched, didn't like loud noises and her habit of repeating things led other children to bully her for being different.

Although it was sometimes difficult for Temple at school, she had an amazing ability to think in ways that others could not. Her brain allowed her to see the world visually, meaning that she could think in pictures. Temple's science teacher, Mr Carlock, could see how clever she was and noticed her interest in science. It was through his teaching and encouragement that Temple's self-confidence soared.

Temple's love for science grew and she went on to study human psychology at college and later gained a doctoral degree in animal science at university.

ACHIEVEMENTS

Temple is now a world-famous professor of animal science, a consultant of livestock and animal behaviour and an autism spokesperson.

Her work with animals and within the farming industry, encouraging better, more humane, handling of livestock, has led to some big changes. By educating companies and their employees on how to take better care of their animals, Temple helped shape and redesign the way livestock is cared for.

Temple overcame a lot of her obstacles through her passion for working with animals. She makes it clear that everyone is different, with unique minds and individual ways of working. Temple often speaks up for the autistic community to promote better education systems and understanding of those living on the autistic spectrum.

Temple invented the squeeze box. This is a machine that gives cuddles and helps to comfort people with autism when they are stressed, angry or anxious about things. Whilst people with autism don't usually like to be held or hugged, they do find the feeling of pressure helps reduce stress. Because of Temple's research, many more things have been created and are available to help people with autism, like weighted blankets.

What is autism?

Autism is known as a neurodevelopmental disorder, which simply means that the brain of someone with autism is wired a little bit differently. Someone with autism is now considered to be on the 'autistic spectrum' as symptoms can vary from person to person, ranging from mild to severe.

The signs of autism usually appear in early childhood and stay with a person for life. Symptoms can include communication difficulties, repetitive behaviour and a sensitivity to noise and activities happening around them. Being in social situations may also prove difficult for someone with autism.

For some people on the autistic spectrum, autism allows them to see things in ways others cannot: maybe the ability to think in pictures, or having a photographic memory and possibly being highly intelligent.

"No one will understand you. It is not, ultimately, that important. What is important is that you understand you."

Matt Haig was born in Sheffield, England on July 3rd, 1975.

Matt had always had an active social life; busy school and college schedules, and many other adventures kept him occupied. He didn't realise until he was in his mid-twenties that maybe he had, in fact, been trying to avoid growing up and entering the adult world. What was his future going to be like? What would happen next? Matt did not know, he felt lost and his mood began to sink.

A wave of internal panic swept over Matt, followed by a black cloud of depression. Matt didn't know how to help himself, he couldn't even find the words, nor the energy, to express what was happening, even to those closest to him. He had never felt like this before and it felt very scary.

Matt had felt sadness before, he had felt worry, but this new feeling was different. This seemed to be taking over everything: every feeling and every thought. It took over Matt's life for quite some time. He couldn't shake it off, he just felt empty. Matt couldn't spend another minute living like this, he needed to find a way out of this dark place.

Helped by his partner, Matt was encouraged to speak to a doctor. She had seen and supported Matt at his lowest points, but unless Matt wanted to make a change and find the energy to help himself, there was little more she, or any doctor, could do to help lift his depression. Matt was diagnosed with having panic disorder, depression and anxiety; he was offered medication to help him with his mood. Matt refused the medication but did accept that a change was needed. With more sleep, time to read, an exercise routine and the love and support of those around him, he was able to find ways to help himself. Within a year Matt was feeling a little better and he understood he would have to be a lot more aware of his moods. He took up writing as a way to express his thoughts and feelings.

Writing became something Matt found extremely therapeutic. He realised that without having gone through his depression in the way he did, he may not be the person he is today. Matt now has a better understanding of his mental health, the things that can trigger his depression, and different ways of coping through difficult times. Matt often speaks publicly about depression, the importance of getting help and supporting others who are fighting their own battles.

ACHIEVEMENTS

Once a man wondering what his future had in store for him, Matt is now happily married with two children and a dog. His work as a novelist, children's book author and non-fiction writer has won him many literary awards. He has sold over one million books in the UK and his work is often on the international bestseller charts. His memoir, *Reasons To Stay Alive*, has been translated into over forty different languages. In his book, Matt shares his journey with depression but also, most importantly, his journey through the darkness to finding the light again.

Having chosen to be open about his mental health problems, Matt is now seen as a champion of mental health issues; desiring to change the way people understand mental health. His goal is to help encourage people to give mental health the same respect and understanding as physical health, treating them both with equal importance.

What is depression?

Depression is a mental health disorder, affecting a person's mood, sleep, motivation, concentration, behaviour, appetite and energy. A person with depression has a deep feeling of sadness and emptiness which takes over their whole body. Depression ranges from mild to severe and may require treatment in the form of psychotherapy or medication. In some cases urgent medical intervention and support may be required.

Women are twice as likely to have depression as men, but men can be more susceptible to its life threatening behaviours. Depression can affect anyone at any time.

"Without imperfection, you or I would not exist."

Stephen Hawking was born in Oxford, England on January 8th, 1942.

Born during World War Two, Stephen was the eldest of four children. His parents believed in good education and his father hoped that Stephen would become a medical doctor.

However, biology and medicine didn't interest Stephen. He enjoyed mathematics and was able to work through problems with exceptional ease. As it came naturally to him he spent very little time actually studying.

Stephen wanted to study Maths, but with that option unavailable at his university of choice, he chose to go into physics. After completing his physics degree, Stephen was awarded first-class honours and decided to further his studies.

Stephen went on to the University of Cambridge to study Cosmology: the science and study of the universe, stars and deep space. It was during this time that Stephen began to notice some strange things happening to his body. At times he felt he was not totally in control of his body movements, finding himself stumbling and occasionally slurring his words. Stephen wasn't too worried at first, but with his health deteriorating, he went to see a doctor and was eventually diagnosed with Lou Gehrig's disease. He was only twenty-one years old, and was told that he probably only had three more years left to live.

Stephen lived well past his three-year life expectancy. He continued his studies, got married and had three children. His health continued to deteriorate, but this did not stop Stephen living his life to the full. The disease eventually paralysed him, meaning he couldn't move on his own and needed a wheelchair, and support in doing things like washing and eating. Stephen lived in his brain and this part of his body never failed to amaze everyone. Stephen completed his studies and went on to become Professor of Physics at the University of Cambridge.

In 1985, Stephen lost his ability to speak. A fellow scientist stepped in to develop a device that would enable Stephen to talk electronically by using a touchpad. Stephen was able to continue his work and share his ideas and theories with the world. To this day, Stephen's computerised voice is recognisable to nearly anyone who hears it.

ACHIEVEMENTS

Stephen surprised his doctors by living fifty years longer than any of them expected. During this time, he gained his PhD and travelled the world visiting universities and science conferences to give lectures. Stephen also made sure he had time for his family.

Stephen became a world-famous cosmologist, theoretical physicist and author, winning awards, medals and prizes for his work. He wrote many important papers on his theories on blackholes, relativity and space-time; his theory that black holes release radiation led to this radiation being named Hawking Radiation.

His life story was turned into a film: *The Theory of Everything*.

Stephen Hawking's most successful book, *A Brief History of Time; From the Big Bang to Black Holes* was written for people with no scientific background or understanding of cosmology. His book offered an easy-to-understand explanation of the complex world of how the universe was made, the concept of time, space and the forces.

What is Lou Gehrig's disease?

Lou Gehrig's, also known as ALS, is a type of motor neurone disease, a non-contagious neurological disorder. Special nerves, called motor neurones, that carry messages from your brain and spine around your body, stop working properly. The muscles in your body weaken and eventually stop working. It also affects the ability to speak, but it does not affect your senses: sight, smell, hearing, taste and touch. Most people diagnosed with ALS are over fifty years old with a life expectancy of only five years. Ninety percent of all cases are non-hereditary.

NAOKI HIGASHIDA

"Everybody has a heart that can
be touched by something."

Naoki Higashida was born in Kimitsu, Japan on August 12th, 1992.

When Naoki was born, he was just like any other baby. As Naoki developed, everything seemed normal, but when he began to try to communicate, no words came.

Naoki was diagnosed with non-verbal autism by the time he was five years old. Being unable to speak was very difficult for Naoki, but soon after his diagnosis he was introduced to an alphabet grid: a tool for helping non-verbal people communicate.

Not being able to speak or converse didn't mean Naoki couldn't think. He would often try to speak but found that when he opened his mouth the words were just not there.

Many people accepted his silence and assumed Naoki wasn't connected to the outside world, when in fact he, like many others with autism, had a whole other world inside his head. Naoki liked to observe the people around him. He watched their expressions and their body movements, finding it fascinating that people could know their own mind and have the power to act in the right sort of way.

If Naoki were to sit with a group of people laughing, he would be so interested in the sound of their laughter and their facial expressions that he would sometimes forget to laugh, leaving people thinking he did not understand the joke. It was often the case that he was very much amused but was so focused on what everyone else was doing, he would not react.

Being non-verbal can be very frustrating, especially when you have something to say. Naoki wanted to share his story and what living in his world was like. By using his communication board and computer, Naoki discovered a passion for writing.

At thirteen years old, Naoki wrote his first book. It was soon published in Japan to great success. A couple who had a child with autism themselves discovered Naoki's story. They were so impressed with the new insight it gave them, that they decided to help translate the book into English. This allowed Naoki's book to get onto the mainstream market, so people across the world could read it.

ACHIEVEMENTS

Naoki is now one of the most famous writers in Japan. His work was not only translated into English, but is now enjoyed worldwide, in thirty different languages.

Naoki's first book *Reasons I Jump* answered fifty questions that people with autism frequently get asked. Questions such as 'Why do people with autism struggle to make eye contact when talking?' and 'Why do autistic people like to line things up, such as toy cars?'. Each word was painstakingly typed out by Naoki using his communication board. He wanted to help people understand what it is like to be living with non-verbal autism, opening a door to a world that is usually shut off to neurotypical people.

Naoki wrote a second book about living with non-verbal autism, giving a new insight into the challenges he faces as a young adult. The book is called *Fall Down 7 Times Get Up 8; A Young Man's Voice from the Silence of Autism*. He has won a number of awards for his work, including best memoir and autobiography.

What is non-verbal autism?

Non-verbal autism is a type of autism that makes it difficult for a person to communicate, whilst also living with the other symptoms of being on the autistic spectrum, such as heightened sensory awareness and repetitive behaviour. It is not known why some people on the autistic spectrum do not develop a full range of language skills.

Whilst language skills, including simple phrases, can develop with the help of speech therapy and further development of social skills, communication still proves difficult for those living with non-verbal autism. Help with communication is also possible with sign language, picture cards and digital communication boards.

# NKOSI JOHNSON

1989 - 2001

"We are all human beings. We are normal. We have hands. We have feet. We can walk. We can talk. We have needs just like everyone else. Don't be afraid of us. We are all the same."

Nkosi Johnson was born in Dannhauser, South Africa on February 4th, 1989.

Nkosi was born with a disease called HIV. His mother had been a carrier of the disease whilst she was pregnant and it had been transmitted to Nkosi whilst he was growing in her womb.

Aware that her ill health may prevent her from being able to care for Nkosi, they went to live in a shelter, known as the Guest House: a place that supported people battling HIV/AIDS.

The Guest House unfortunately had to shut, and aware that her health was so poor, Nkosi's mother asked the shelter owner, Gail, if she would continue to care for and look after Nkosi. He would need a lot of medication and treatments to help him manage the disease, and if he was living with Gail, hopefully she could continue to provide it. Nkosi's mother passed away a few years later.

Nkosi was growing up well in Gail's care; she wanted to provide him with a normal life. But when his application to start school was denied due to his illness, Nkosi found himself having to fight for the right to go to school. Nkosi was interviewed by local news channels, his case was even being talked about by the government. Three months later, a new law was passed: no school could deny a place to a child with HIV/AIDS, and workshops would be available to help educate teachers and parents about the disease.

Nkosi still wanted to help people understand what it was like growing up as a child with HIV. He was invited to talk at an International AIDS convention. Standing in front of ten thousand people and with cameras televising his speech around the world, Nkosi made the world stop and listen.

Together Nkosi and his adoptive mother Gail fundraised so that they could open a place similar to the Guest House where they first met. Its focus would be on supporting women and children living with the disease. They called it Nkosi's Haven.

ACHIEVEMENTS

Although Nkosi passed away at the age of twelve, he managed to get the world to pay attention to the HIV/AIDS crisis in Africa. Nkosi took his powerful speech to another HIV/AIDS conference in America and was called an inspiration by South Africa's president at the time, Nelson Mandela.

Nkosi was awarded the first ever International Children's Peace Prize. The prize was dedicated to him after his death, and the statuette has been named after him. The 'Nkosi' is now awarded each year to the winners of the prize: other children who have stood up, and made a change in the world.

Nkosi's story was turned into a book: *Care For Us And Accept Us*. Another book, *We Are All The Same: A Story Of A Boy's Courage And A Mother's Love* was also written by Jim Wooten about Nkosi's journey and mission to help the world understand HIV/AIDS.

What is HIV/AIDS?

HIV is a virus that attacks the white blood cells in the body. The white blood cells are responsible for the immune system and protect the body from germs and infections. If left untreated HIV can turn into AIDS, which is when the immune system has been so badly damaged by the virus, the body is no longer able to defend itself from infections and disease. Treatments are available to help those living with HIV, but there is currently no cure available.

HIV/AIDS cannot be caught from holding hands, hugging or kissing another person with the virus. It lives in the affected person's blood and body fluids and is only passed on to another if their body fluids or blood enter another person's own system.

FRIDA KAHLO

1907 - 1954

"Feet, what do I need them for if I have wings to fly."

Frida Kahlo was born in Mexico City, Mexico on July 6th, 1907.

Frida was born in a little blue house, where she was raised with her six sisters. She would often prefer to sit and draw rather than play.

At the age of six, Frida caught a disease called polio, which nearly killed her. Luckily for Frida she was strong and recovered, but it left her right leg weakened and with a limp. Frida's father encouraged her to do a lot of sports to help strengthen her leg as much as possible. She swam, played football, and even wrestled, something that was very uncommon for girls to do at the time.

As Frida grew older she hoped to become a doctor, but at eighteen, whilst in medical school, she was badly injured in a traffic accident. She broke her back, ribs, pelvis, leg and foot, and dislocated her shoulder! Being so badly injured meant Frida was bedridden and would have to stay in hospital to recover.

Frida's mother, knowing Frida's childhood passion for art, brought in some paints and an easel to the hospital so that Frida would have something to do whilst she recovered. It was during this time that she rediscovered her love of art and decided she would waste no more time in pursuing a career in medicine. She would be an artist!

Feeling confident about her talent, she took her work to an artist she admired to seek his advice on becoming an artist herself. He ended up not only falling in love with her work, but also with Frida. He supported Frida's dream, encouraging her to take her painting seriously.

Frida used her art as a way of expressing herself. The accident meant she was living with chronic pain. This was something that would stay with her for the rest of her life and was often highlighted in her work.

Frida lived her entire life in the blue house where she was born. The house is now a museum, which many people visit from all over the world to see all Frida's personal belongings still on display.

ACHIEVEMENTS

Frida is a world-famous artist. Of all the paintings she created, fifty-five of these were self-portraits. She was very proud of her Mexican heritage and would often exaggerate her eyebrows and facial hair whilst wearing beautiful, brightly coloured traditional Mexican clothing and jewellery, with flowers in her hair.

Her paintings stood out against traditional art. They weren't like anything seen before. Frida told her story through art, not letting her pain define her, or deter her from embracing her uniqueness.

Each colour Frida used held a different thought or feeling, which she noted down in a journal. Green symbolised good, warm light. Navy blue was to show distance, but also tenderness. Yellow was madness, sickness and fear but also represented the sun and joy. Frida's work was inspired by Mexican folk culture and the Aztecs.

What is chronic pain?

When someone lives in constant pain for three to six months or more, this is known as chronic pain. Some people live with chronic pain for their whole lives.

The pain leaves the person feeling very tired and uncomfortable. It not only affects them physically, but also affects their mental health.

It is difficult to understand what it is like to have to live with chronic pain, but many people have found a way to manage their pain and continue to lead normal lives with the help of physiotherapy, medicine and support from others.

HELEN KELLER

1880 - 1968

"The best and most beautiful things in the world cannot be seen or even touched, they must be felt with the heart."

Helen Keller was born in Alabama, USA, on June 27th, 1880.

Helen was born a healthy baby. She learnt to say her first words early and was also quick to walk.

Just before Helen's second birthday she became very poorly with a fever. Helen eventually pulled through but her mother noticed that Helen wasn't reacting to her waving her hand across her face or responding to noise around her. The doctors confirmed that the fever had left Helen both blind and deaf.

Helen grew up alongside Martha, the daughter of the family's cook. The girls created more than sixty different signs, similar to sign language, to communicate together. Helen still struggled to communicate and understand the world around her, which left her very frustrated and prone to having tantrums.

Helen's mother was constantly looking for answers and ways in which she could help her daughter. She stumbled across the successful education of another deaf-blind child, filling her with hope that Helen would achieve the same.

The family enlisted the help of a special teacher, Anne Sullivan. Anne had experienced temporary blindness herself and could appreciate the struggles of living in darkness. She was determined to help Helen.

By spelling out words on Helen's hand she tried to get Helen to find the connection between the word and an item in front of her. The day came when Helen understood her first word. By spelling out the word 'water' on Helen's hand, and then running water over her hands, Helen now had her first word!

Helen learned to speak placing one hand on Anne's voice box and the other hand on her lips. By feeling the vibrations of her voice and feeling the movement of her lips, Helen was able to use her own voice to mimic the vibrations and create words.

By the time Helen went to the Cambridge School for Young Ladies, in preparation for college, she could use a number of communication methods: touch lip reading, braille, spoken word, typing and finger spelling. Helen went on to become the first deaf-blind person to earn a Bachelor of Arts degree.

ACHIEVEMENTS

Helen went on to publish twelve books, her first being an autobiography called *The Story of My Life*. As an advocate for blind and disabled people, Helen traveled to thirty-five different countries around the world, sharing her story and trying to help as many poor and blind people as she could.

Helen founded Helen Keller International, a global charity that was set up to help veterans from World War One who were left blinded. It is still open today and continues to help millions of vulnerable people living with blindness and malnutrition around the world.

Helen featured in a silent movie called *Deliverance*, which told the story of her life and the help she received from her teacher. Many more films have been made to share Helen's fascinating story including a drama, a documentary and an animated children's cartoon.

What is deaf-blindness?

Deaf-blindness is a condition whereby someone has both a hearing and sight impairment. Also referred to as 'dual sensory loss' or 'multi-sensory impairment'. As with being blind or deaf, the condition doesn't mean someone is always totally blind or deaf; they may have variable loss of both senses.

Deaf-blindness causes difficulties with communication and mobility. The support available varies from person to person, depending on the degree of the impairment. Braille, touch cues, lip reading, guide dogs and hand-on-hand sign language are all tools used to help those with deaf-blindness communicate and integrate.

MALATHI KRISHNAMURTHY-HOLLA

"My self-confidence is not paralysed."

Malathi Krishnamurthy-Holla was born in Bengaluru, India on July 6th, 1958.

When Malathi was only a year old, she became quite ill. A fever raged throughout her body and she was diagnosed with polio. When the fever subsided, Malathi was left paralysed from the neck down.

Her family did all they could to help find a treatment, and to help strengthen her body. For two years she was given electric shock treatment in hospital, which, with time, helped restore some of the strength and movement in her upper body. However, the treatment didn't work on her legs, leaving her in need of a wheelchair. Malathi was moved to a specialist orthopaedic hospital, where they continued to do a further fifteen years' worth of treatments and surgeries to try and help improve her condition.

Malathi would spend much of her time wishing she could run with her friends, or have wings to fly like a bird. It saddened her to think she'd be unable to run and she most definitely didn't have wings to fly. Determined not to give up on her dreams, she kept going: one day she would find her way!

By the age of sixteen Malathi had undergone thirty-two different surgeries. She felt there had to be another way to help distract her from the pain. Medication could help, but she wanted something more. She decided to take up sport.

Alongside her sports training, Malathi wanted to get a good education. On her first day at college, she discovered that her classes were inaccessible, with no lifts between the different floors of the building. Not being one to let things stand in her way, Malathi convinced the college to move all her lessons to the ground floor so she could continue her studies.

Keen to keep up with sports alongside her studies, Malathi signed herself up to a local athletic competition. Upon arrival she found that no other females had put their name forward in her category. The organisers were keen for her to withdraw. Malathi again refused to quit: she wanted to be given the chance to compete, and she didn't care who it was against. Malathi ended up competing against eight men and she won!

ACHIEVEMENTS
Malathi went from strength to strength with her athletic abilities and represented her country in the Paralympics Games, the World Championships, the Asian Games, the Commonwealth Games and the World Masters. She has won over four hundred and twenty-eight medals!

Her talent stretched over many track and field sports including shot-put, javelin, discus and both the 100 metre and 200 metre race. Malathi is still one of the fastest female Indian athletes in a wheelchair.

Being so successful with her sporting achievements, she was awarded the Padma Shri civilian honour and the Arjuna Award for her services to sport for her country.

Malathi started her own foundation, The Mathru Foundation, in Bengaluru. The foundation's mission is to help teach physically disabled people to overcome their difficulties. The main focus is to help those who have had polio. The foundation helps children from poor, rural areas, providing treatments and inspires them to chase their dreams.

What is polio?

Polio, otherwise known as poliomyelitis, is a highly contagious viral disease. The virus attacks the nervous system and causes muscle wastage and paralysis and can in some cases be fatal. There is still no cure, but treatments are available to treat the symptoms and provide support.

Polio is spread through contaminated water or food and from being in contact with another infected person. Although young children are more at risk of catching polio, due to better awareness of the disease and immunisation programmes, polio cases have dropped by ninety-nine percent, and in some countries, polio has been completely eradicated.

DENNA LAMBERT

*"Until you embrace the idea of no limits,
you don't know what might be possible."*

Denna Lambert was born in Arkansas, USA.

Denna grew up in a neighbourhood that was very poor and suffered a lot of violence. She was also visually impaired. Denna's visual impairment had been inherited from her father's side of the family, something called congenital cataracts.

Despite Denna's visual impairment, she attended a regular school and often went to a special summer school for the blind, giving her hope for a positive and normal start in life.

Denna did well at school and wanted to pursue a degree in electrical engineering. Some of the colleges which Denna applied to were only just starting to be more diverse and inclusive. Denna faced difficulty in being accepted into her college of choice, not only due to her disability, but also because of her race.

With patience, perseverance and the grades she needed, she was eventually awarded a place to study, going on to earn a degree in science and general business administration management.

Finding work would be her next challenge. Many companies were wary of employing a visually-impaired person. She spoke with her college career service counsellor about her worries and found herself speaking at a conference for students with disabilities, highlighting the problems she and others faced. Little did Denna know that a recruiter from NASA was sat in the audience that day. They liked what she had to say and were keen to offer her a job.

Denna started work for NASA with specially adapted technology to help her complete her tasks and communicate with others in her team. It only took Denna a year at NASA before she was given the opportunity to really make a difference to those she had spoken for in the conference back at college. Denna was promoted to Disability Program Manager for NASA. This role gave her the opportunity to make the changes needed to help support disabled employees and adapt the work environment to make it more accessible for any future employees who identified as disabled.

ACHIEVEMENTS

Denna worked at NASA as the Disability Program Manager for nine years, providing her expertise in diversity and inclusion in the workplace. By making sure there were equal opportunities available and that employment laws were followed, it allowed the employment of more minority groups and disabled people within NASA.

During the Mars Rover Mission, where two robots were sent to explore the planet Mars, Denna requested the modification of the work environment, to give better accessibility for all. This allowed disabled students to come and see the progress of the mission and give them a front row seat of all the action.

Denna also volunteered as a Girl Scout troop leader. She was in charge of planning group activities for the development of her unit. She spent her time giving her troop different enrichment opportunities, to build their experience, knowledge and confidence and gain valuable life skills.

What is blindness?

Blindness is an inability to see anything, sometimes not even light. Some people can be considered 'legally blind' which is a term used for those living with a vision impairment ranging from having very limited vision to complete blindness. If a person is not able to read the top letter on the opticians' chart with the strongest eyeglass correction, they are considered 'legally blind'.

There are many different causes of blindness: genetics, disease, injury and other occular complications due to health problems. For people with severe impairment, and those who are blind, the help of guide dogs, braille and other technology can help them adapt to their disability.

◯⫶◯ JONO LANCASTER ◯⫶◯

"With the right attitude you can achieve anything."

Jono Lancaster was born in Leeds, England on October 31st, 1985.

Thirty-six hours after Jono's birth, he was abandoned at a social welfare clinic. Jono had been born with something called Treacher Collins Syndrome; his facial features and bones hadn't formed properly as he developed in the womb.

Jono needed someone to care for him and give him the attention and love that all newborn babies required. He was placed with a foster carer called Jean. Upon holding Jono, Jean felt an immediate bond. With so much love for this little baby she had only just met, Jean went on to adopt Jono and raise him as her own.

Being raised in a loving family environment provided Jono with the best possible start in life. It was only when Jono started school that he noticed he didn't look like everyone else. The kids at school could be very mean, making fun of his appearance and running away from him.

As a teenager, things were sadly no better. Jono found himself often in trouble at school. It was easier if people were talking about his behaviour and not focusing on the way he looked.

By his late teens, Jono was feeling very low. Years of bullying had left him with low self-confidence. Unsure of who to turn to, he kept his troubles to himself. He didn't want to have to tell his mother how unhappy he was, in case it left her feeling she had failed him in any way.

A friend stepped in and offered Jono an opportunity to work with him in a bar. Jono was terrified, but, much to Jono's surprise, he found himself really enjoying his work. Everyone was really friendly and he wasn't met with any judgement. This gave Jono the confidence to achieve his own goals. He gained a diploma in Sports Science and hoped to start work as a fitness instructor.

Jono got himself a job in a local gym. He found that the more he built his relationships with colleagues and customers, the less self-conscious he felt. Treacher Collins wasn't holding him back from being successful, so Jono made the decision that it would not hold him back in any other area of his life either.

ACHIEVEMENTS

Jono devotes his time to helping others with his condition, by travelling the world to meet families who have children with Treacher Collins. He offers families the chance to ask questions and learn more about what it is like growing up with the condition. Jono leads anti-bullying workshops, his core message being acceptance of others and all our differences. He is also an ambassador for the charity Jeans for Genes, which raises money to support families who have children living with genetic disorders.

Jono founded the Love Me, Love My Face Foundation to help provide relief to people with Treacher Collins and other cranio-facial conditions and their families. The Love Me, Love My Face Foundation aims to give advice and financial support for essential medical care to families who most need it. It promotes worldwide education, better knowledge and understanding of cranio-facial conditions.

What is Treacher Collins Syndrome?

Treacher Collins Syndrome is an extremely rare genetic disorder, present from birth, that affects the formation and development of the head and face.

The gene that is responsible for supplying information on how the bones and tissues should grow as a baby develops in the womb has a fault. The effects of Treacher Collins can vary from mild to severe. There is no cure for Treacher Collins, but people living with the condition may need to use hearing aids, have speech therapy and may have the option of reconstructive surgery.

"Creative people are sometimes fortunate enough to be able to incorporate their most traumatic experiences into their art."

Matt Lucas was born in London, England on March 5th, 1974.

As a small child Matt didn't always have it easy. He had hayfever and asthma and his skin was covered in scratches from itching his eczema. His eczema and asthma were an inconvenience, but they didn't define Matt, he was always up for fun and games with his peers, even if it was sometimes a little hard to keep up with them all.

Matt would often find his mind wandering. At four years of age, he found himself in trouble. Out on a day trip with his parents, Matt lost sight of them whilst he was distracted by everything else going on around him. Feeling worried, he finally spotted his parents across the road, up ahead. Without thinking, he dashed over to them. Forgetting about the road, Matt was hit by a car. He was extremely lucky to escape unharmed.

Two years passed by and something strange started to happen. Matt woke up one morning to find his pillow was covered in hair. Not overly concerned at first, Matt woke up day after day to find more and more hair on his pillow. Eventually, all of Matt's hair fell out.

The doctors thought the hair loss could be a delayed reaction to the accident he had had two years previously and it was something called alopecia.

Matt stood out, being a bald seven year old, and found himself being pointed at and stared at, sometimes also being called names.

Matt tried out wigs for a short time to see if that helped but he found them scratchy and far too hot and bothersome to wear. It was easier to embrace his baldness and learn to deflect any negative comments with humour.

It wasn't until Matt's adult life, when retelling the story of his accident to a doctor, that they explained his alopecia wasn't just down to the shock of the accident, but was an autoimmune disease. By this point Matt had outgrown his self-consciousness about his appearance and had found a way to use his baldness and sense of humour by starting a career in the entertainment industry.

ACHIEVEMENTS

Matt attended a national youth theatre and it was here that he met the person who would become his writing partner. Together they created a British comedy series that made fun of the silly things that happened in England. Matt and his co-writer, David Walliams, went on to create a number of comedy programmes which rocketed them to fame. Matt has appeared in many different television shows, once in a game show as a large baby! He has also been cast in films, most noticeably, his role as Tweedle Dee and Tweedle Dum in *Alice in Wonderland*.

Matt never intended for his acting career to end up with him being on the big screen. He believed that, in order to be a serious actor, you had to be able to show your talent on stage, not just in front of a camera. It is Matt's wish to one day write a successful musical.

What is alopecia?

Alopecia is an autoimmune disease that affects both men and women equally. You cannot catch alopecia, but it can appear at any age. It is thought that people may develop alopecia from trauma, stress, after battling a virus or in some cases there may be no known cause at all.

The chance of getting alopecia is higher if someone else in your family has the condition. There is, as of yet, no cure for alopecia and it affects people differently. The cells in your body, which are responsible for attacking viruses and germs become confused and attack the hair follicles, the part of your body that produces hair.

HANNAH OLATEJU

"Be you, be free, be fabulous."

Hannah Olateju was born in London, England in May 1999.

Hannah was just like any other toddler, curious and full of energy, but then, she became ill. Her parents gave her some medicine, but her condition was rapidly declining, forcing them to take her to the local hospital. Hannah was admitted immediately as a rash had started to spread across her little body. She was diagnosed with meningococcal septicaemia, a severe case of meningitis, which poisons the bloodstream.

Hannah needed a lot of medicine and care over the weeks that followed, her chance of survival was pretty low. The doctors made sure they did everything they could to save her. Hannah's condition gradually improved, but she wasn't out of danger. She now had gangrene in all four limbs. The only way to stop the infection spreading would be to amputate both arms below the elbows, and both legs below the knee.

Hannah spent the next year in hospital, recovering and learning how to use prosthetics to help her mobility. Her family were delighted when she was well enough to return home.

Growing up without limbs was normal for Hannah, she was so young when she had the amputation that she couldn't remember what it was like to have them. Children at school attempted to bully Hannah, but her mother had encouraged her to always choose kindness over negativity, and Hannah refused to listen, or take note of any of negative comments.

As a teenager, Hannah found herself suffering from low self-esteem and low self-confidence, normal for any girl her age. This all changed when she was taken on a holiday to Jamaica with her family. Hannah found herself surrounded by people of all shapes and sizes, embracing and loving themselves the way they were. By the time she returned home, the free-spirited Jamaican attitude had rubbed off on Hannah. She started to make videos and take photos and post them online, sharing make-up tutorials, her fashion choices and her hair styles. She soon found herself with many fans, supporters and followers on various social media platforms, all in awe of her confidence, positivity and bubbly nature.

ACHIEVEMENTS
Hannah has around two hundred thousand followers across her social media channels. With this success, Hannah started up her own company, Hannah & Co.

Her company hopes to empower people to have self-confidence, feel good about their body and learn to love themselves. Hannah runs workshops for individuals and businesses to help show them make the most of their social media platforms. She also offers life skills, leadership and body positivity programmes that can be used in schools to encourage teenagers to feel positive about their choices for the future and to be kind to themselves. Hannah is currently working towards achieving her business degree and is having a break from her social media accounts.

Hannah's make-up tutorials on her Instagram and YouTube account were a way to inspire people, especially other amputees, to continue to love themselves and allow themselves to feel beautiful. Hannah wants people to understand that although beauty comes from the soul, you can still be bold, beautiful and shine.

What is meningitis?

Meningitis is an infection that affects the protective membranes that cover the brain and spinal cord. The infection causes inflammation, which can be life threatening if not treated as soon as possible.

The two most common causes of meningitis are viral and bacterial infections.

Treatment is determined on what strain of meningitis the person is carrying. Immediate treatment is needed to reduce the risk of the infection spreading to the blood, causing further damage around the body and increasing the risk of gangrene.

Meningitis can be contagious, but there are some preventative measures in the form of vaccinations.

"Being happy isn't the same as being perfect – it's learning to live with imperfections."

Adam Pearson was born in London, England on January 6th, 1985.

When Adam was five years old, he bumped his head. A bump formed on the spot where Adam had knocked his head, but instead of it healing and disappearing, as bumps usually do, Adam's bump stayed put. He was diagnosed with having a condition called neurofibromatosis.

Adam spent a lot of time in hospital to monitor his condition, but he was never overly concerned by the diagnosis. His parents believed it was best to focus on getting on with life and making sure Adam had the care he needed.

Adam was growing up with a facial disfigurement at a time when many schools didn't have effective anti-bullying programmes in place. There was not much empathy or understanding for someone living with a difference. This meant Adam was subjected to bullying and name calling from many of the children at school.

Adam learnt that the best way to deal with the hurtful comments was to reply with something quick and witty. If he didn't react as expected, the bullying wasn't so much fun, and so the bullies eventually backed off. The name calling still hurt, but Adam didn't want to give them the satisfaction of seeing that.

Adam underwent many operations throughout his childhood, often at Great Ormond Street

Children's Hospital in London. It was on one of his visits that he spotted a poster for Changing Faces, a charity that campaigns to help and support people with visible differences.

The charity worked with Adam on coping strategies; how to deal with reactions and behaviour towards him and how to diffuse situations that made him feel uncomfortable or unsafe. By building his confidence and self-esteem, Adam learnt that it was sometimes ok to not always be ok.

Adam went to university to study Business Management and gained his degree. He found himself a job, working for an English television broadcaster. Adam has worked on, and presented, a number of programmes that highlight the lives of people living with disabilities.

ACHIEVEMENTS

Now an award-winning disability rights campaigner, actor and presenter, Adam has won, and been nominated for, various awards for his work across the board. He even starred in a movie alongside Scarlett Johansson, which he hoped would change the way people perceived those living with a disfigurement.

He is an ambassador for three different disability charities, Us On A Bus, Jeans for Genes and The Childhood Tumour Trust. He continues to campaign for better policies and systems at school to prevent bullying, especially for those living with disabilities and differences.

Adam never considered a career in acting. As a teenager, his greatest wish was to pass his exams and find a girlfriend. However, he did know that whatever he was going to do, he wanted to make sure he could find a way to help others like himself; campaigning for equality and diversity for people with disabilities.

What is neurofibromatosis?

Neurofibromatosis is a genetic condition that affects the nervous system. This genetic disorder causes tumours, usually non-cancerous, to grow on nerve tissue in or on the body.

There are three different types of neurofibromatosis. Each type affects different age groups and has different symptoms and effects on the body. It is thought that most cases are inherited, but sometimes the condition can just appear in early childhood with no previous history of it in the family. Neurofibromatosis is not contagious and although treatment and surgery may be available, there is currently no cure.

"It's not until you need to be strong that you find out how strong you really are. And I think everyone is just as strong and powerful, they just never get tested."

Turia Pitt was born in Tahiti, French Polynesia on July 24th, 1987.

Turia was a very sporty child. She and her brothers would often play outside as they had no television at home. As well as being athletic, Turia was bright and intelligent, doing well at school. She developed an interest in engineering and followed that interest through school and on to university. Turia gained a double degree with honours in engineering and science.

Whilst studying, being active was still very important to Turia. In 2011, she signed herself up for an ultra-marathon, having been offered a free place from the organisers. The ultra-marathon was a hundred kilometre run across the Australian outback!

The day of the ultra-marathon arrived. However the organisers had failed to warn the runners of the potential bushfire hazard further along the course.

A few hours into the race, she and the other competitors became aware of smoke and literally had to run for their lives. A few of the runners, including Turia, found there was no escape. They were surrounded by fire!

When help finally arrived, Turia was airlifted straight to hospital. She had severe burns on over sixty-five percent of her body and was put straight into an induced coma for six months, so the doctors could try to save her.

The doctors were overjoyed when Turia awoke. One of the doctors said he had never seen anyone with that degree of burning survive. She lost seven fingers and had tissue damage and scarring all over her body from the burns. She would have to go through over two hundred operations and would spend the next two years in recovery, having to relearn how to walk, how to dress herself and even how to feed herself.

Turia was determined to exceed the doctor's expectations and regain her independence, with the goal to lead a normal life.

ACHIEVEMENTS
Despite being told that she may never walk again, with a lot of therapy and training, Turia not only walked, but learnt to run again.

After a lot of rehabilitation Turia was ready for a challenge. She signed herself up to compete in an Australian Ironman competition, another endurance race. After successfully competing in the race, she signed up to The World Ironman Championships in Hawaii!

Turia is now a motivational speaker; her mission is to inspire others to never give up, despite what life throws at you and to work hard on achieving your dreams.

Turia is the author of a number of books. Her memoirs, *Everything to Live For* and *Unmasked*, talk about the accident, her recovery and her life now. Her third book, *Good Selfie*, a book targeted at teenagers, talks about discovering your own self-worth, self-confidence, following your dreams and how to help yourself through difficult times.

What is a burn?

Burns are skin damage from heat, the sun, friction, chemicals or electricity. A burn ranges in pain and in its seriousness. Most burns can be treated by running lukewarm water over the affected area for twenty minutes and by keeping it clean. More severe burns require medical attention.

A first-degree burn is the most common burn, usually very mild, causing redness and pain to the outer layer of skin. Second degree burns affect the outer layer of skin and the layer underneath, causing swelling, blisters, redness and potential scarring. Third degree burns are the most serious, damaging or destroying a deeper level of tissues and reaching the fatty layer. This leaves severe scarring, numbness and requires surgery.

DANIEL RADCLIFFE

"The fact that some things are more of a struggle will only make you more determined, harder working and more imaginative in the solutions you find to problems."

Daniel Radcliffe was born in London, England on July 23rd, 1989.

Daniel was an only child. His mother worked as a casting director for the BBC and his father was a literary agent. Being born into a creative family, it was no surprise to them that aged five, Daniel declared he wanted to be an actor when he grew up.

School wasn't particularly fun for Daniel; he was quite clumsy, a slow reader and writer, and was often told by his teachers that he was stupid. When Daniel's mother heard what the teachers were saying, she marched straight into his school to confront them! Daniel was different, but his vocabulary was way above that of his peers, he just struggled with his motor skills. Things such as tying his shoelaces, swimming and even riding a bike proved challenging for Daniel.

At seven years of age, Daniel was diagnosed with having dyspraxia. After years of being called stupid, he had started to believe that he probably was. Daniel was chatty, socially awkward, disorganised and found it difficult to sit still in class and concentrate on the tasks given to him. His dislike for school grew as he got older, when he found himself struggling to keep up with his classmates in writing and reading. He felt disheartened, everything he tried to accomplish he failed at, and it seemed he lacked any sort of talent in any academic field, when actually, it was probably just down to a lack of understanding and support for his dyspraxia.

Determined to help Daniel build his self-confidence, his parents decided to let Daniel explore his interest in acting. He was soon asked to audition for a part in a BBC production of *David Copperfield*. The producers, impressed with Daniel's charm and easy-going nature, cast him in the role of young David Copperfield over the other more experienced child actors.

After this success, Daniel was keen to keep acting. His parents were wary of his desire to go into the world of acting, having had experience with it themselves. However, Daniel insisted this was what he really wanted to do. Not long afterwards, at the age of eleven, Daniel found himself auditioning for a role in an adaptation of a very famous children's book.

ACHIEVEMENTS

Daniel was lucky enough to know some of the people who were already cast in this new film, having worked with them previously. He had the right experience, looked the part, and was soon given the lead role of Harry in the film adaption of *Harry Potter and the Philosopher's Stone*. Daniel went on to play Harry Potter in all eight movies, winning many awards for his performance, stretching over eight years of filming.

Once the filming of *Harry Potter* was complete, Daniel decided to take some time to explore acting on stage. He performed many different shows on New York's Broadway and London's West End. Alongside his stage career, Daniel continues to work in the film industry.

Despite his earlier struggles at school with reading and writing, Daniel enjoys expressing his creativity by writing short stories and poetry. Being an actor, Daniel felt he was often just using another person's voice, and he wanted to share his own. At seventeen years old, he created the pen name of Jacob Gerson, and he published four of his own poems.

What is dyspraxia?

Dyspraxia, otherwise known DCD (Developmental Coordination Disorder), is a neurological disorder. Dyspraxia usually runs in the family and is three to four times more likely to develop in boys than girls, with mild to severe affects.

People with dyspraxia usually have trouble with their motor skill coordination; things such as running, tying shoelaces, drawing and writing may prove more difficult. Dyspraxia may also affect a person's sensory and social responses.

Treatment or therapy for dyspraxia is available with ergotherapy, occupational therapy, physical therapy, speech therapy and language therapy options.

ADALIA ROSE

"I try my best to make people smile."

Adalia Rose was born in Texas, USA on December 10th, 2006.

A few weeks after Adalia come into the world, doctors noticed she wasn't growing at a normal rate for a newborn baby. She was still very small and this concerned them, they decided that they would run some tests to try and determine the cause.

At three months old, Adalia's mother was given the news that her daughter had something called progeria. The diagnosis would mean that Adalia would grow up with a number of complications, and her life would potentially be cut short by the condition. It wasn't long after the diagnosis that she could start to see the changes in her daughter due to the effects of progeria.

A decision was made by her mother and stepfather that they were going to give Adalia the best life they possibly could and to not dwell on her diagnosis. They did not want Adalia to be scared about what the future may bring, but instead concentrate on the here and now, and the experiences they would create together as a family.

A Facebook page was set up to help track Adalia's progress. She and her family would create short videos of their daily lives, and as she grew older, of Adalia doing her make-up, or singing and dancing. None of them were prepared for how quickly Adalia's fanbase would grow. She started to receive hundreds of encouraging messages from fans near and far; people couldn't get enough of her bubbly personality!

The videos brought a whole new level of understanding of progeria to the world. Adalia regularly films videos with her mother, where they talk about normal teenage life, Adalia's hospital appointments or medications she is taking.

Adalia shares that she still has sad days, or days when she stumbles across messages that aren't so supportive or nice, but tries to concentrate on all the love and support she gets from her family and friends. Some days she says that although it would be nice to just be like her friends, she also enjoys the fact she owns so many fancy wigs, and that she can rock a different hair style every day whilst her friends are stuck with the hair they have.

ACHIEVEMENTS

Adalia has never let anyone stop her from spreading joy to others. She is continuously encouraged by all the positive messages she receives from around the world, especially from kids who are going through a tough time themselves, thanking her for bringing them so much happiness.

Adalia is now a social media superstar! Her YouTube, Facebook, Twitter and Instagram accounts attract millions of fans. She also manages her own lifestyle website with the help of others who are keen to support her in sharing positive stories from many different people: messages of love, family and inclusivity.

Adalia has been paid to do promotional videos to discuss her condition and to call for more action in the research into finding a cure. She and her family have made sure to donate their fees to help fund scientists to do more research about the condition, finding better medication and looking for a cure.

What is progeria?

Progeria Syndrome, otherwise known as Hutchinson-Gilford Progeria Syndrome (HGPS) is a very rare genetic condition. It is so rare that there are thought to be under five hundred cases worldwide. Progeria is not an inherited condition, and as of yet, there is no cure.

Due to the aging effects of progeria, a person living with the condition will have limited growth, loss of body fat and hair. Their skin will appear aged and they will have a stiffness of joints. Although their exterior may appear older, their mind is not affected by the condition.

SADAKO SASAKI

1943 - 1955

"I will write peace on your wings and you will fly all over the world."

Sadako Sasaki was born in Yamaguchi, Japan on January 7th, 1943.

Sadako's country was in the midst of war at the time of her birth. Sadako's father joined the army and was sent away to fight for their country, whilst her mother stayed home to continue to look after her.

Sadako was two years old when an atomic bomb was dropped on Hiroshima, not far from where they lived. Sadako and her mother were home at the time and the blast was so great that it blew Sadako out of the window. Miraculously, Sadako survived unhurt. With their house destroyed, Sadako's mother picked her up and ran, whilst radioactive dust fell from the sky.

Everything was destroyed from the bomb blast and Sadako and her family had to go and live with a relative in another town. It was another month before the war ended.

Everyone had to work hard to try and rebuild their lives after the bomb, and Sadako returned to school.

At the age of ten, Sadako started to get dizzy spells, and her family noticed a decline in her health. Their local clinic was unsure of the cause of her illness and sent her to the hospital for further tests. The results of the tests showed that Sadako had leukemia, most probably caused by the exposure to radiation from the bomb. Her family were told to prepare for the fact she may only have a year to live and that Sadako would have to stay in the hospital and start receiving treatment.

It was very boring in hospital, but Sadako and some of the other patients were inspired to start making origami paper cranes. In Japan, it is believed that if you fold a thousand paper cranes, your wishes will come true. Sadako spent a lot of her time folding cranes whilst receiving her treatment. Each time she made a paper crane, the nurse would dutifully hang it up for Sadako around her hospital bed.

ACHIEVEMENTS

Sadako's brother claimed that she was able to achieve her goal, even exceeding it, but unfortunately her illness was too great and she passed away in her sleep. Sadako was buried with a thousand paper cranes.

Students, saddened by the death of their classmate, decided to form The Paper Crane Club to honour her. Another 3,100 schools, from Japan and overseas, donated money for a monument to be built in Sadako's memory. The Children's Peace Monument is located in the centre of the Hiroshima Peace Park, near to where the bomb was dropped. Thousands of people visit the monument each year, leaving paper cranes at its feet.

Sadako would make paper cranes out of any paper she could find. Only having a small supply herself, she would sneak into other patient's rooms and ask them to keep any gift wrapping they received, or wrapping from medical equipment. Some of her school friends would occasionally bring in extra paper on their visits from school or home.

What is leukemia?

Leukemia is cancer of the blood, which affects the white blood cells and bone marrow in your body. The bone marrow starts to produce abnormal white blood cells, these unhealthy white blood cells are unable to fight infections, which is the normal role of healthy white blood cells. The red blood cells, which are responsible for carrying oxygen around your body, are also affected.

It is not known what exactly causes most cases of leukemia. You cannot catch it and it is not hereditary. Medication and treatment is available to help manage the symptoms.

ELLIE SIMMONDS

"If you've got a disability, you're normal - it's just something that's different."

Ellie Simmonds was born in Walsall, England on November 11th, 1994.

Ellie was born with a condition called achondroplasia, a condition that her older sister, Katie, has too.

Aware that she and her sister were of shorter stature, her parents made it clear that having achondroplasia wasn't something that would hold either of them back. They believed that it wouldn't benefit either Ellie or her sister if they received special treatment. They would make sure they always had the same opportunities to succeed as everyone else.

Ellie was lucky enough to have a swimming pool at home and was often found splashing about and swimming with her siblings. She was a strong swimmer and it wasn't long before her parents decided that she could do with some training to teach her more than the basics. At the age of five, Ellie started swimming lessons.

Her skills quickly improved and she was able to keep up with all the able-bodied children in her swim class and by the age of eight she was ready to take part in her first swimming gala. Ellie didn't win anything, but she loved the atmosphere and buzz of the competition.

She was invited to join a programme for talented child athletes, and with a more intensive training programme Ellie was, at the age of nine, soon achieving the same finish times as the eighteen-year-old disabled swimmers.

Ellie and her mum made the hard decision to move to Swansea, away from the rest of her family during the week, so she could train with other young swimmers. She wanted to compete professionally and be considered for a place on the Paralympic team. With half of her family living so far away it was hard, but Ellie had a chance, and her parents wanted to give her that chance.

Ellie was fast! She was like a rocket in the water. Even at her young age she was beating the older, more experienced swimmers at the club. With such raw talent, strength and speed, Ellie was chosen to represent Great Britain in the Paralympics by the time she was thirteen, making her the youngest on the team!

ACHIEVEMENTS

Ellie, at thirteen years of age, made her debut at the Beijing 2008 Paralympic Games, competing in the 50 metre, 100 metre and 400 metre freestyle, 50 metre butterfly and the 200 metre individual medley. She won gold medals for both the 100 metre and 400 metre freestyle, and went on to receive the 2008 BBC Sports Personality of the Year award!

By 2009, Ellie was bringing home even more gold medals and this time received an award from the Queen of England, who gave Ellie an MBE. She was the youngest person in history to be given an MBE. This award has since been upgraded to an OBE.

Ellie volunteers with the Girl Guides, otherwise known as Girls Scouts. She is one of the group leaders and helps organise activities for the girls in her unit. Her unit gave her the leader name 'Aqua Owl', in reference to her swimming achievements. Ellie is also an ambassador for the Scout Association.

What is achondroplasia?

Achondroplasia is the most common form of dwarfism, which affects approximately one in every twenty-five thousand births. It is a genetic disorder that may be inherited from a parent who is carrying the gene responsible for achondroplasia. A protein found inside the gene responsible for the growth and structure of a person's bones and tissues is mutated. This mutation has an impact on the development of the bones, which causes a person with achondroplasia to be born with shorter limbs and be shorter in height.

Achondroplasia is usually diagnosed before birth. Treatment is available to help with any complications.

MATTIE STEPANEK

1990 - 2004

"We must remember to play after every storm."

Mattie Stepanek was born in Maryland, USA on July 17th, 1990.

Mattie was the fourth child born to Jeni Stepanek. Two of his three other siblings had passed away from a very rare and fatal form of muscular dystrophy. Mattie and his surviving older brother had also been born with the same condition.

Jeni had been unaware she was a carrier the condition herself and had passed it on to her children.

Mattie was a very bright young man, with a love of reading and writing from a very early age. When his older brother passed away from complications of the condition, Mattie began to record his own poetry on a tape recorder, to help him process his brother's death. By the age of five he would begin to write his thoughts on life down himself, no longer needing the help of his tape recorder.

Due to his muscular dystrophy, Mattie had to spend much of his time in the local children's hospital. Despite this, he was determined to be grateful for each and every day he had, and shared his uplifting positivity with everyone around him. Mattie was an inspiration to everyone that met him, from the doctors and nurses who treated him, to the television stars who invited him on to their show to discuss his poetry.

His poetry was his way of sharing his 'heartsong'; the thoughts and feelings he had deep inside him, the words he felt he needed to share with the world.

Mattie was incredibly clever and by the age of eight he was being home schooled. He was academically advanced, but his health was gradually worsening. He continued to write his poetry and started public speaking alongside learning at home.

When Mattie wasn't sharing his messages of hope and peace, he was busy being a regular kid; reading every book he could get his hands on and enjoying playing with Lego®. He encouraged people to celebrate their lives, no matter the obstacles, and continued to hope that a cure would be found for his condition. Mattie passed away just before his fourteenth birthday.

ACHIEVEMENTS

Mattie became a *New York Times* bestselling author with his book of poems *Journey Through Heartsongs*. Seven bestselling books full of his poetry and peace essays have now been published. He became just as famous for his motivational speaking. Mattie won many awards for his writing, as well as for his advocacy for peace, notably winning the 2007 Independent Publisher's Peacemaker of the Year Award. A park was dedicated to Mattie in Rockville, Maryland: 'Peace Park'. A life-size bronze statue of Mattie and his service dog sit in the centre, and a number of his most notable quotes are found around the park.

After Mattie passed away, his mother continued to spread his message by working with the We Are Family Foundation's Three Dot Dash Global Teen Initiative. The programme works with children aged thirteen to nineteen, encouraging cultural diversity and mentoring on how to share their voices, promoting a positive vision for the future and the changes they wish to see in the world.

What is muscular dystrophy?

Muscular dystrophy is a rare group of over thirty different genetic disorders that weaken the skeletal muscles, which help control movement. Each disorder has a different effect on specific muscle groups, varying symptoms and severity. The long term effects of a person's muscles weakening will have an effect on their mobility and level of disability.

Muscular dystrophy is caused by a lack of a particular protein, which is responsible for the function and the structure of a person's muscles. Muscular dystrophy is an inheritable disease, and although there is yet no cure, there are treatments that help ease the symptoms and prevent complications.

MADELINE STUART

"Have fun and believe in yourself."

Madeline Stuart was born in Brisbane, Australia on November 13th, 1996.

Madeline was born with Down's Syndrome. Down's Syndrome may present some challenges, but this was not something that was going to stand in Madeline's way.

In 2015, Madeline's mother took her to a fashion show in their hometown of Brisbane. Seeing everyone up on stage was amazing. Madeline, who has limited speech, loved the show and made it very clear that she too wanted to be a model.

Her mother knew that it would be tough, but if this was something Madeline really wanted to do, she would support her and help her achieve her goal.

With her new dream in sight, Madeline wanted to ensure that she lived a long and healthy life. She discovered a love for gymnastics, dance and cricket, hobbies that would help her keep fit and healthy. Both the fitness and fashion industries were lacking in diverse role models and Madeline was ready to step up and fill that gap.

A photoshoot was arranged for Madeline. This was the first time she would have her hair and make-up done professionally. It was also to be her first experience posing for the camera. Madeline had a fantastic time and was even more determined to pursue a career in modelling. Madeline and her mother proudly posted the photos on her social media account. By the next morning she found her photos had been shared worldwide, making her an internet sensation! She was offered representation by a modelling agent and was soon in high demand. People in the fashion industry were recognising Madeline and were keen to book her for their runway shows and for photoshoots all around the world. Madeline had made it. She was a model!

Creating diversity in the fashion industry, especially for those living with disabilities, was something that Madeline and her mum wanted to focus on; they wanted to see a permanent change in the industry. Madeline wanted to be treated the same as every other model, including getting paid properly and fairly for her work.

ACHIEVEMENTS

Madeline became the face of change for diversity in the fashion world. She made it clear that she would work just as hard as anyone else; fighting for equal rights, and inclusion of disabled people within the fashion industry.

Madeline has since become the first professional model with Down's Syndrome. She has walked some of the biggest and most famous runways around the world: Paris, New York, London, China and more! Continuing to show the world that she is committed and professional, Madeline has worked hard for her place on the runway, and in beauty campaigns, breaking down the barriers for people with disabilities and taking the fashion world by storm!

Madeline has her own fashion label called 21 Reasons Why. In February 2017, Madeline took to the stage at New York Fashion Week, sporting her very own collection of clothes, designed to mirror her own sense of style; bright, fun, comfortable and easy-to-wear pieces.

What is Down's Syndrome?

Down's Syndrome is a genetic disorder which is present before birth. Our bodies are made up of pairs of chromosomes which carry the genetic information needed to create life. Most people have twenty-three pairs, totalling forty-six. But for a baby born with Down's Syndrome, there is an extra chromosome, so they have forty-seven instead of forty-six.

Down's Syndrome can affect intellectual and learning abilities, growth and speech. It varies in range from mild to severe. People with Down's Syndrome may also have problems with their thyroid or heart.

MATT STUTZMAN

"Never say never. If I can do this with no arms, anything is possible."

Matt Stutzman was born in Kansas City, USA, on December 10th, 1982.

Matt was a healthy baby, but he had been born with no arms. The doctors explained there was no medical reason he had no arms, it just occasionally happened. Feeling unable to support a child with disabilities, Matt's parents decided to put him up for adoption. At thirteen months old, Matt was adopted into the Stutzman family.

It was decided that Matt was to be treated like any other kid; growing up as part of a large family, everyone had their fair share of chores to do, without exception. If Matt wanted to do something, he was encouraged to give it a go. He had the freedom to try anything, even climbing trees. Matt understood that if he got up there by himself, he needed to work out how to get down too. It was important that Matt found a way to problem solve and consider how he could take on different tasks.

As Matt grew up, he continued to do things alongside his family and friends, including learning to drive a car, going shooting and having a family of his own. But, unfortunately for Matt, other people were quick to judge his abilities and he found it almost impossible to find an employer who would give him a job. Matt attended interview after interview, but no one wanted to hire someone with no arms. Feeling saddened by the lack of opportunities to support his family, he found himself depressed and unsure of his future.

One day a programme came on the television about archery, it gave Matt an idea. If Matt couldn't get a job to support his family, he realised there was another way he could put food on the table. He would take up archery!

Matt's archery equipment arrived. He looked up tips and tricks online on how to use his bow and arrow with no arms. After much scouring on the internet, Matt discovered a video tutorial that offered him some advice. Within two days, using his legs and with a lot of practise, Matt was able to use his bow and arrow with ease.

ACHIEVEMENTS

Matt entered his first competition in February 2010. He was the only person there with a disability, but he finished the day having won some prize money. Matt started to practise eight hours a day and continued signing up for various competitions. He was encouraged to try for a place on the US Paralympics team and found himself travelling to the London 2012 Paralympics, where he won a silver medal.

In 2015, under the watchful eyes of a Guinness World Record adjudicator, Matt attempted to shoot the farthest accurate shot with a bow and arrow: a distance of 283.47 metres. After missing his first shot, he tried again and hit the target. To this day no one has broken Matt's record, able-bodied or disabled.

As a professional motivational speaker, Matt often uses humour as a way to address his difference to the audience. Matt discusses that even though there may be limitations to what you can do, there are no limitations in trying. With the right mental attitude, anything is possible unless, of course, that anything is vacuuming, changing dirty nappies or washing the dishes.

What is a birth defect?

Birth defects, also known as congenital disorders, are present from birth, ranging from mild to life threatening. Birth defects can appear internally, externally and in chemical imbalances in the body, affecting people physically, mentally and intellectually. Around three percent of all births will be affected by some form of birth defect. Around seventy percent of all birth defects have no medical cause.

As there are so many different types of birth defects and levels of severity, each case will have its own treatment. Types of birth defects include the absence of limbs, Down's Syndrome, birth marks, cleft lip or cleft palette, heart defects and Spina Bifida.

"I have Asperger's, it means I am sometimes a bit different from the norm, and given the right circumstances, being different is a superpower."

Greta Thunberg was born in Stockholm, Sweden on January 3rd, 2003.

At eight years of age Greta was doing a project in school about the effects of climate change. During the discussion, a short film was shown to explain the impact humans were having on the planet. Greta could not stop thinking about what she had seen. Greta had been diagnosed with Asperger's at a young age, this meant that sometimes Greta found herself hyper-focusing on subjects or things which interested her or caused her concern. Not understanding why others were not as upset as she was about the issue, she became completely overwhelmed with concern about climate change and temporarily stopped talking at the age of eleven. Her parents were concerned about her and tried to encourage Greta to use her voice again, for if she chose not to speak, how could she share her worries with others? How would she be able to ask for change?

A change was needed and to make an impact, Greta knew she needed to get her message to the people in power: those running the country. Her parents warned Greta that her plan may not be met with support, she may find the reactions to her protest were not the reactions she was hoping for. But, she was strong and determined; if she didn't stand up for climate change, who would?

Greta tried to get her teachers and friends to join her in a protest outside parliament, but no one was interested. She sat alone, with a hand painted sign which read 'School Strike for Climate Change' in Swedish and handed out flyers with facts about climate change. She posted pictures of her protest on social media and found her posts drawing attention from local journalists, who went to ask what her protest was about.

Greta returned for a second day of protesting, expecting to spend another day sat alone. Much to her surprise, a few other people had turned up to join her. From then on, each day Greta returned to protest, even more people arrived, ready to support her cause.

Greta realised then that she could make a difference.

ACHIEVEMENTS
School Strikes for Climate Change became a global movement. 1.6 million people across 128 countries around the world gathered in various towns and cities on Friday March 15th, 2019, to strike for climate change. This became known as the 'Fridays for Future' movement.

Greta delivered a speech, in English, in front of thousands of people at a climate rally that day. She also travels the world, using climate-friendly transport, to spread awareness of how climate change is affecting the planet. *Time* magazine named Greta 'Person of the Year' in 2019 and one of the world's '100 Most Influential People'. She was also nominated for the Nobel Peace Prize.

Greta travelled to America, by boat, to spread her climate crisis message. Aware of the amount of carbon emissions an aeroplane put into the atmosphere, she looked for an alternative way to travel. It took her and her team fifteen days to travel from Plymouth, England to New York, America.

What is Asperger's?

Asperger's, now known as ASD, Autistic Spectrum Disorder, may affect a person's ability to communicate, socialise and fit into social norms.

People with ASD tend to be above average in intelligence and are likely to find themselves hyper-focused on things they see as important or interesting to them. The cause of ASD is unknown, although it is thought to be genetic and possibly hereditary. People with ASD may find speech therapy, physical therapy, behavioural therapy and, in some cases, medication useful. Boys tend to be diagnosed more frequently than girls due to the fact that girls find it easier to mask their symptoms.

HARRIET TUBMAN

1820 - 1913

"Every great dream begins with a dreamer. Always remember you have within you, the strength, the patience and the passion to reach for the stars and change the world."

Harriet Tubman was born into slavery in Maryland, USA in March 1820.

Harriet's exact year and date of birth was never truly known, which was quite common for a lot of people who were born into slavery. In the 1800's many Black people were forced into slavery by rich families, making them work on their land, and in their homes, without any pay.

By the age of six, Harriet was loaned out to another slave owner and his wife to help take care of their baby. Harriet's job was to watch the baby while it slept. Should the baby wake up crying, Harriet would be beaten as punishment. Harriet worked hard for her slave owners, in their home and on their plantation throughout her childhood. There was little time for family and friends.

At the age of twelve, Harriet got in the way of a slave owner throwing an iron weight at another slave. The iron weight hit her hard on the head and nearly killed her. Harriet was strong and survived the injury, but it left her having fits and black outs. She would have epilepsy for the rest of her life. Harriet was still expected to keep working alongside the other slaves, despite her injury and her epilepsy.

Harriet dreamt of a better life for herself. She had heard of other slaves escaping and making a break for freedom. The states in the north had outlawed slavery, and a system known as the 'underground railway' was created. The underground railway wasn't a real railway. It was a series of routes, or 'lines', and safe houses known as 'stations', that would lead slaves, or 'passengers', to safety. The conductors were volunteers: abolitionists, both Black and white, who believed slavery was wrong and wanted to help others escape.

Movement along the underground railway was dangerous, as those escaping ran the risk of being caught by slave catchers. Most journeys were carried out at night, when there was less chance of being seen. Harriet wasn't afraid. She wanted her freedom and knew if she could gain it, she would be able to help others do the same.

ACHIEVEMENTS

Harriet gained her freedom! After her escape, Harriet felt saddened by the family and friends she had left behind. She needed to find a way to get back and help them gain their freedom. Harriet decided to volunteer as an underground railway conductor. She became so successful at guiding slaves to freedom that a reward was offered for her capture.

Slave owners were angry that their slaves were going missing and soon it became too dangerous for Harriet to continue conducting her work. Over ten years, Harriet safely guided and freed many people, earning her the nickname 'Moses'.

Harriet continued to fight for the freedom of others, volunteering during the American Civil War to serve as a nurse and a spy. By the end of the Civil War, slavery throughout America was banned. A biographical film was made about her life in 2019, named, simply, *Harriet*.

Harriet Tubman's birth name was actually Araminta Ross, 'Minty' for short. She was also given the nickname 'Moses' during her years as an underground railway conductor, because just like in the story of Moses, Harriet delivered her people from slavery.

What is epilepsy?

Epilepsy occurs when the brain has seizures and stops sending the right information around the body. A person may have epilepsy due to genetics or a brain injury or damage.

Someone having an epileptic seizure may lose consciousness and shake. They will not realise this is happening to their body. The best way to help someone having a seizure is to make sure they aren't in any danger of hurting themselves, clearing any hard or sharp objects out of their way. It is also advised to make sure their airways are kept clear by putting them in the recovery position once the jerking has stopped.

KING GEORGE VI (WINDSOR)

1895 - 1952

"The highest of distinctions is service to others."

King George VI was born in Norfolk, England on December 14th, 1895.

Born Prince Albert Frederick Arthur George Windsor, he was fourth in line to the throne at birth.

Albert was a very anxious and sensitive child who suffered from ill health. He had a condition called 'knock knee' whereby his knees were angled inwards. He wore corrective splints to help straighten his legs.

Growing up at a time when children were 'seen and not heard' was tough for Albert. It was common amongst wealthy, high society families to hire nannies and home help to keep the children out of the way of the adults.

Not only did Albert feel anxious about the lack of attention from his parents, but in his private lessons he was made to feel inadequate again, when his tutors told him he wrote with the wrong hand! A myth at this time was that writing with your left hand was bad, and many believed this had to be corrected. Albert was forced to learn how to write with his right hand instead of his left. Under all this stress, he soon developed a stutter.

As Albert grew up, he tried to lead a quiet life alongside his many royal duties. One of his duties as a prince was to make public speeches, something that Albert hated and often struggled with, due to his stutter.

Albert's wife, Elizabeth, suggested finding a speech therapist. She found someone named Lionel Logue who came highly recommended; his breathing and vocal training techniques were quite new but proved effective. Lionel believed that a stammer was not physical, but psychological.

Lionel refused to make any special arrangements for the future king, nicknaming him Bertie and inviting him to undertake therapy at his office rather than in the palace. Albert was given tongue twisters and told to wear earphones, so that he would stop listening to the sound of his own voice. When he was confronted with a word he was unable to say, he was told to sing it instead. With time and patience, Albert soon found his stammer improved.

ACHIEVEMENTS

In honour of his father, King George V, Albert chose to change his name to George, before being crowned King of England in December 1936. He was now known as King George VI.

When World War Two broke out, King George needed to do a radio broadcast to announce that England was going to war. His first official radio address would be broadcast live, as there wasn't the technology to pre-record his speech. Lionel helped prepare the king, marking pauses and suggesting alternative, easier to pronounce words in place of the more complicated ones. King George delivered his speech beautifully, and without stammering.

When George's father, King George V died, George's older brother Edward became king. However, Edward was only king for eleven months after being told he wasn't allowed to marry the woman he loved as she was not deemed a suitable match for a king. Edward chose to pass the crown to his younger brother and follow his heart.

What is a stammer?

A stammer is a speech disorder. This speech impediment is usually recognisable by a person's repetition of sounds and syllables in a word.

There are two known forms of stammer, developmental and late onset. Developmental occurs in childhood and appears whilst a child is developing speech and language skills. Late onset is rarer, but affects older children and adults, maybe due to the result of illness, trauma, injury or a neurological condition.

It is thought that stammering is possibly genetic. Stammers are treated with speech and language therapy and although it is possible to grow out of a stammer, some people find it lasts through adulthood.

NICK VUJICIC

"If you don't get a miracle, become one."

Nick Vujicic was born in Melbourne, Australia on December 4th, 1982.

When the nurse handed Nick to his mother, she went into shock and his father nearly fainted. Nick had been born with an extremely rare condition, known as Tetra-Amelia syndrome. He had no arms, or legs, only two feet and two toes.

It took a while for his mother to get over the initial shock, but she believed it must have been 'God's plan' for her son to be born with this condition and decided that it was now her and her husband's responsibility to love Nick unconditionally.

Nick was one of the first physically disabled students in Australia to attend a state school. Whilst there, he learned how to write, use a computer and operate his wheelchair using his toes. This allowed Nick the opportunity to study and it also gave him the mobility he needed to keep up with his friends.

Nick was bullied by the other children at school, physically, emotionally and mentally. By the age of ten he was feeling very down and upset. He questioned his purpose and what he would be able to achieve in his life. Nick was encouraged to use his faith to help guide him, and with a lot of support and love from those around him he managed to find a way through his depression.

A janitor who was working at Nick's school decided to stop and tell Nick how much potential he could see in him. 'You're going to be a speaker,' he told Nick. He helped him understand the power he had in being able to inspire others. By sharing his story he had the ability to instill hope and courage in people who were questioning their own self-worth.

Nick's first speech was in front of a group of six other students. In giving his speech, he realised that other people also faced their own, different struggles. He felt able to connect with them and inspired them to take a more positive, hopeful outlook on life.

He spoke at many other events and soon went on to become a public speaker.

ACHIEVEMENTS

Nick is one of the world's most popular motivational speakers. By embracing his disability and using his unique experiences he travels around the world to share his story. Nick campaigns for mental health and wellbeing, and is an anti-bullying ambassador.

Nick founded Life without Limbs, an international non-profit organisation and ministry. He also founded another company Attitude Altitude, which offers motivational speaking.

His first book *Life without Limits, Inspiration for a Ridiculously Good Life*, became a bestseller and has been translated into thirty different languages. Nick has also produced a number of motivational films and presented many TED talks.

Nick has a wide range of hobbies and interests. Many people may have thought his condition would limit his ability in participate in these activities, but Nick just thought it would be another fun challenge for him. He is a keen swimmer and surfer, and he enjoys painting and even sky diving!

What is Tetra-Amelia syndrome?

Tetra-Amelia syndrome, otherwise known as Phocomelia, is an extremely rare condition, whereby a person is born with no arms or legs. The bones of the arms and legs are either missing or underdeveloped.

The cause of Tetra-Amelia syndrome isn't fully understood. Scientists have made a link to it possibly being a genetic syndrome or maybe a reaction to certain medication that used to be given to prevent morning sickness in pregnancy. There is no specific treatment for Tetra-Amelia syndrome. Mobility support such as a wheelchair and assistance in daily tasks such as eating and getting dressed may be needed.

"I hope that together, we can create more positive images of disability in the media and in everyday life."

Maysoon Zayid was born in New Jersey, USA in 1974.

Maysoon had a difficult birth. When she was born she did not get enough oxygen, which left her with brain damage. She was later diagnosed with cerebral palsy. The doctors assumed the worst for her, declaring she would probably never be able to walk. Her father wasn't having any of it. As soon as Maysoon was old enough, he'd put her heels on his feet and walk with her to help encourage the motion in her legs and build her strength. Maysoon was able to walk by the time she reached kindergarten.

The day came for Maysoon to start school, but upon seeing her disability, the principal of the school refused her a place, telling her parents that she should be placed in a school for people with special needs. Once again Maysoon's father was not having any of this. He was so angry that he sued the school and made them give his daughter a place. Maysoon's cerebral palsy didn't have any affect on her intellectual abilities, and her father wanted to make sure she got treated as an equal to everyone else. Her family didn't believe in the word 'can't'. Her parents would regularly tell her that no dream was impossible.

Maysoon was a confident and happy child and never realised her differences until she was into her teens. She began to notice that other people treated her differently. She just wanted to be accepted for who she was.

Maysoon dreamed of a career in acting. Yet again, she was met with people saying she couldn't. She found that the very few parts that were available in television and film representing disabled people were being played mainly by able-bodied actors. Maysoon wondered why, when twenty percent of the American population identified as being disabled, these roles weren't being filled by disabled actors. With such limited opportunities, not only for someone with a disability, but also as a Muslim woman, Maysoon knew she'd have to find another way to get herself seen and heard.

ACHIEVEMENTS

With her determined can-do attitude Maysoon decided to step into the world of comedy. Maysoon co-founded and helped produce the New York Arab American Comedy Festival, becoming the first stand up comedienne to perform in Palestine and Jordan.

Maysoon also did a TEDx talk about her cerebral palsy journey titled *I Got 99 Problems, Palsy is Just One*. She continues to work hard against discrimination towards disabled people in television and film and also addresses negativity towards the Muslim community. She has also written and performed an autobiographical book *Find Another Dream*, for Audible.

Maysoon would visit Palestine for up to three months a year to run an arts programme for disabled and orphaned children in refugee camps. Her aim was to bridge the gap between disabled and able-bodied children, and help the children cope with trauma. Her programmes provided training for parents and teachers who were working with disabled children.

What is cerebral palsy?

Cerebral palsy is a group of disorders that affects the movement, muscle coordination, and balance in a person's body. There are different types of cerebral palsy ranging from mild to more severe forms.

Cerebral palsy can be present in pregnancy, at birth, or appear in the first five years of a child's life. There is no one specific cause of cerebral palsy, but it's usually the result of abnormal brain development or damage. Treatment like physical therapy, speech therapy and occupational therapy can help those with mild cerebral palsy lead a normal life. For those with more severe cases, they may require the help and support of a carer.

Glossary

Abolitionists
People that wanted to end and be rid of slavery.

Amputation
Having an operation to remove or cut off part of the body.

Autoimmune
When antibodies in the body, which usually help fight infection and disease, turn on and attack healthy cells within the body.

Blood Cells
There are three types of blood cell, each with different roles:
Blood Cell (White): helps protect the body from infection and disease.
Blood Cell (Red): carries oxygen around the body.
Blood Cell (Platelets): helps prevent bleeding by clotting the blood.

Bone Marrow
Spongy, fatty tissue found inside some bones. Bone marrow is responsible for the production of blood cells.

Cartilage
Tissue found between bones.

Cells
The building blocks which create life.

Chromosomes
The structures that hold the genes (the information) needed to create who we are.

Coma
Deep state of sleep or unconsciousness due to illness, injury or sometimes induced to help recovery.

Donor
A person who donates a body part or blood in order to save the life or help another who is seriously ill.

Eczema
A skin condition that causes itching, redness and irritation.

Genetics
Study of inheritable conditions, or traits, that can be passed down the family line.

Hayfever
An allergic reaction to pollen, grass or other allergens.

Hereditary
A disease or character trait that is passed down through the family.

Impairment
A disability affecting the structure or function of a person's body or mental abilities.

Inflammation
A swollen area in or on the body causing redness, discomfort and pain.

Lumbar Puncture
The removal of fluid from the lower back to test for disease.

Malnutrition
When the body does not get the nutrition needed to be healthy, either from lack of food or being unable to absorb what it needs.

Mental Health
The health of someone's mind and emotional state.

Motor Neurons
Cells that carry messages to and from the brain along the nervous system.

Mutation
A permanent change in a gene which can lead to a disruption in a person's development.

Nervous System
The name for the body's control centre that connects the brain, spinal cord and nerves, sending messages around the body and controlling any body functions.

Neurological
A condition affecting the brain and nerves.

Ocular
Eyes and sight.

Orthopaedic
The treatment and study of the growth and development of bones.

Paralysed
Lack of movement or feeling in part of the body.

Pigmentation
The colouring of a person's skin.

Physiotherapy
A treatment using exercise and massage to help build strength and mobility in the body.

Prosthetics
An artificial body part made to replace a missing limb, hand or foot.

Protein
Complex carriers of important information for body functions and structure.

Psychological
The human mind, thoughts and feelings.

Psychotherapy
Treatment of a mental illness through counselling, behavioural therapy and discussion.

Reconstructive Surgery
An operation that changes or rebuilds part of a body.

Seizures
A sudden attack or illness, whereby a person may lose consciousness and have uncontrollable shaking or convulsions.

Stroke
Reduced or blocked blood flow to the brain, resulting in the death of brain cells.

Therapy
A treatment intended to help someone build up their strength, mentally or physically, to recover from injury or illness.

Thyroid
A small organ, otherwise known as a gland, in your neck which helps control the way the body works and grows.

Transplant
A medical operation that moves an organ or part of one human body to another.

Trauma
A distressing or upsetting experience or physical injury.

Vaccinations
An injection treatment that helps build immunity to certain diseases.

About the author: Louise Gooding

Louise is a children's author, based in a small village in Switzerland.

After several years running a children's entertainment business Louise decided that she wanted to pursue a career in children's writing. She has an interest in sharing stories that discuss many important and sometimes difficult and neglected subjects, particularly those that are rarely discussed with children. Because Louise sometimes struggled at school, she is keen to teach children that we are all unique individuals and it is important to be understanding, be kind and to respect everyone and celebrate our differences. *Just Like Me* is her debut book.

Growing up, Louise was a bit of a character. She had great parents who loved reading to her and always encouraged her creativity. She was the loud, bubbly, over-the-top friendly, troublemaker at school. I'm sure there are many of her old teachers who upon hearing her name would say 'Oh gosh, I remember her, how could I forget! She was a bright girl, very creative but…'. There was always a BUT…

She was a bit much for some kids, definitely a bit much for the parents of those kids, but the teachers, for the most part, were pretty great. Some teachers just didn't get her or know how to settle her down and keep her focused on work, and some even believed that Louise wasn't worth bothering with, much to her parents' frustration.

As an adult, Louise is still a character, just a bigger, older version of her younger self. She is impulsive, often chaotic and disorganised, but very creative. When she really believes in a project, she tends to hyper-focus on it until she collapses in a heap of exhaustion at the end.

It wasn't until her youngest daughter started having the same problems at school that Louise herself had experienced, that she realised something maybe wasn't quite right. When her daughter had an assessment for ADHD, it was suggested Louise consider getting assessed too.

Throughout her assessment a lot of things started to make sense. Louise had grown up being labelled and judged by others, but had she just been completely misunderstood? ADHD in the 1990s wasn't a big thing. Parents and teachers weren't really aware of its existence.

Because of her own personal experience Louise understood the importance of building her daughter's self-confidence. She told her it was ok to be different, to embrace who she is and to find a way to make it a strength.

In writing this book, Louise set out to find diverse role models with interesting stories. It was important, not only for her youngest, but for her other children too. Her eldest had been diagnosed with having mild Asperger's and had been through her own ups and downs at school, and her middle daughter had discitis at the age of two, which had left her living with chronic back pain, and needing physiotherapy and pain medication for many years.

Louise's research led her to discover people she had never heard of before, people she felt needed to have their stories heard. There were so many amazing people who, despite their perceived differences or potential limitations, had achieved fantastic things. So why didn't we know their stories? Why didn't we know who they were? Louise's children couldn't be the only children out there who would benefit from discovering these amazing people. And so, the book began...

About the artists

Angel Chang

Angel Chang is an illustrator from Taiwan. She was born with a sensitive heart and is drawn to observe connections between all manner of things. With unique ways of using colours and compositions, Chang's artwork often radiates both her wild imagination and sophisticated observation at the same time. After her many psychotherapy appointments, she has knowingly lived with her high-functioning autism symptoms for two years now.

Angel's clients included Chronicle Books, Macmillan Publishers, *The Washington Post*, *National Geographic*, etc. Her first illustrated picture book *Most of the Better Natural Things in the World* has been longlisted in the World Illustration Awards 2020.

Caterina delli Carri

Caterina delli Carri was born in Puglia, in the south of Italy.

She has always loved to draw. Since she was a child, she invented stories and put them on paper, she designed characters and used to draw everywhere in her grandfather's country house. She was enchanted looking at picture books to catch every little detail.

When she was nineteen she moved to Rome and then Turin to study Visual Arts and Set Design at The Academy of Fine Arts.

Caterina's works are inspired mostly by nature, everyday life, old photos and childhood memories. She loves to take care of even the smallest details within an illustration.

Currently she lives in the Tuscan countryside where she works on educational books, magazines, children's books and drawings for different clients around the world.

Melissa Iwai

Melissa Iwai is the children's book author and illustrator of *Soup Day* and *Pizza Day*. She has illustrated over thirty picture books during her career, including most recently, *Thirty Minutes Over Oregon* by Marc Tyler Nobleman, Clarion 2018 (An Orbis Pictus Honor Book for Outstanding Nonfiction 2019 and Junior Library Guild Selection). She lives in Brooklyn with her husband, author Denis Markell and their teenaged son.

Dante Gabriel Hookey

Dante Gabriel Hookey is a queer, autistic, non-binary illustrator-author from England who now lives in Texas.

They graduated with a BA(Hons) in Illustration from Falmouth University, and have since helped make a kid's show for the BBC, designed gifts with LUSH and worked with many other clients worldwide.

Dante Gabriel Hookey is inspired by surrealism, dreams, mysticism, manga and the resilience-brilliance of autistic, trans and LGBT+ people.

By translating their experiences and inner world into art, especially narrative and comics, they hope to show others they're not alone in being 'different'!

Dante Gabriel Hookey is also involved in LGBT+ advocacy work and writes a blog on mental health and art.

They're currently writing and illustrating a poetic comic about a monk's relationship with an artist and designing an oracle deck of common creepy crawlies.

Quotes

In order of appearance:

Bettis, Jerome, 2011, *Jerome 'The Bus' Bettis rolls in*, Patrick Gavin, Politico. Available at https://www.politico.com/story/2011/12/jerome-the-bus-bettis-rolls-into-dc-070422 (accessed 17 June 2020)

Biles, Simone, 2016, *How August Cover Star Simone Biles Blazes Through Expectations*, Sade Strehlke, Teen Vogue. Available at https://www.teenvogue.com/story/simone-biles-summer-olympics-cover-august-2016 (accessed 17 June 2020)

Bolt, Usain, 2017, *A Conversation with Usain Bolt – The World's Fastest Man*, Vikas Shah MBE, Thought Economics. Available at https://thoughteconomics.com/usain-bolt-interview/ (accessed 22 June 2020)

Branson, Richard, 2008, *Buy Gatwick? Why not?*, Decca Aitkenhead, The Guardian. Available at https://www.theguardian.com/business/2008/sep/20/branson.interview (accessed 22 June 2020)

Braun, Ralph, 2010, *Rise Above: How One Man's Search for Mobility Helped the World Get Moving*, The Braun Corporation

Brown-Young, Chantelle, *Vitiligo: A Skin Condition not a Life Changer*, thosegirlsarewild, 7 Jul. Available at https://www.youtube.com/watch?v=__3Hm14whUY (accessed 22 June 2020)

Chandran, Sudha, 2016, *In conversation with dancer Sudha Chandran*, Yoshika Sangal, Governance Now. Available at https://www.governancenow.com/views/interview/in-conversation-dancer-sudha-chandran (accessed 22 June 2020)

Chiu, Connie, 2020, *Connie Chiu, Singer and Model*, Albinism OHCHR. Available at https://albinism.ohchr.org/story-connie-chiu.html (accessed 22 June 2020)

Cohen, Brad, 2008, *Front of the Class: How Tourette Syndrome Made Me the Teacher I Never Had*, VanderWyk & Burnham, U.S.

Cox, Kadeena, 2017, *Kadeena Cox: "MS doesn't put a full stop after your name"*, Multiple Sclerosis Trust. Available at https://www.mstrust.org.uk/news/views-and-comments/kadeena-cox-ms-doesnt-put-a-full-stop-after-your-name (accessed 22 June 2020)

Davis, Warwick, 2019, *Star Wars actor Warwick Davis visits schoolboy sharing his condition to help raise awareness of dwarfism*, Shufflebotham, Bethan, Stoke Sentinel. Available at https://www.stokesentinel.co.uk/news/local-news/star-wars-actor-warwick-davis-3467506 (accessed 22 June 2020)

Fotheringham, Aaron, 2020, *Wheelz Aaron Fotheringham*. Available at https://www.aaronfotheringham.com/about/ (accessed 22 June 2020)

Gomez, Selena, 2020, *Selena Gomez On Recapturing Her Public Image*, Mental Health And Her No. 1 Album, Garcia-Navarro, Lulu and Balaban, Samatha, National Public Radio. Available at https://www.npr.org/2020/01/26/799389965/selena-gomez-on-recapturing-her-public-image-mental-health-and-her-no-1-album?t=1590668220999&t=1592830018961 (accessed 22 June 2020)

Grandin, Temple, 2012, *Different... Not Less*, Future Horizons

Haig, Matt, 2013, *The Humans*, Canongate Books

Hawking, Stephen, 2010, On *Into The Universe*, Discovery Channel

Higashida, Naoki, 2014, *The Reason I Jump*, Sceptre

Johnson, Nkosi, 2000, Aids Conference Durban

Krishnamurthy-Holla, Malathi, 2014, *She found the answer to pain, paralysis and pity. Now she shares it with others*, Velayanikal, Malavika, Your Story. Available at https://yourstory.com/2014/02/malathi-holla-paralysis (accessed 22 June 2020)

Lambert, Denna, 2020, *Meet Denna Lambert, Program Manager at NASA*, American Foundation for the Blind. Available at https://www.afb.org/research-and-initiatives/employment/meet-denna-lambert (accessed 22 June 2020)

Lancaster, Jono, 2015, *Jono Lancaster Fights Treacher Collins Syndrome With Attitude*, Lewis, Ricki (PHD), DNA Science. Available at https://dnascience.plos.org/2015/10/29/jono-lancaster-fights-treacher-collins-syndrome-with-attitude/ (accessed 22 June 2020)

Lucas, Matt, 2009, *This much I know*, Husband, Stuart, The Guardian. Available at https://www.theguardian.com/lifeandstyle/2009/jun/28/matt-lucas-comedian-interview (accessed 22 June 2020)

Olateju, Hannah, 2020, *Hannah & Co Blogs*. Available at https://hannah.cnddigital.com/ (accessed 22 June 2020)

Pearson, Adam, 2018, *Adam Pearson: 'If I'd been born into the social media generation, things would have been completely untenable'*, Silverman, Rosa, Telegraph. Available at https://www.telegraph.co.uk/christmas/2018/12/02/adam-pearson-born-social-media-generation-things-would-have/ (accessed 22 June 2020)

Pitt, Turia, 2020, *Stepping into your power with Turia Pitt*, Bodman, Rebecca, Business Chicks. Available at https://businesschicks.com/turia-pitt-real-life-superhero/ (accessed 22 June 2020)

Radcliffe, Daniel, 2014, *21 Random Questions With Daniel Radcliffe*, WSJ Staff, The Wall Street Journal. Available at https://blogs.wsj.com/speakeasy/2014/10/28/21-random-questions-with-daniel-radcliffe/ (accessed 22 June 2020)

Rose, Adalia, 2017, *Q & A BULLIES THINK AGAIN!*, Adalia Rose, 12 March 2017. Available at https://www.youtube.com/watch?v=FOfV43jMQis (accessed 22 June 2020)

Sasaki, Sadako, inscription under the Sadako Sasaki Peace Garden, La Case de Maria, Santa Barbara

Simmonds, Ellie, 2012, *Ellie Simmonds: 'If you've got a disability you're normal'*, Channel 4. Available at https://www.channel4.com/news/ellie-simmonds-paralympics-golden-girl (accessed 22 June 2020)

Stepanek, Mattie, 2014, *How Mattie Stepanek's Words Inspired Millions | The Oprah Winfrey Show | Oprah Winfrey Network*, OWN, 22 June. Available at https://www.youtube.com/watch?v=ZxD-U1rY0vw (accessed 22 June 2020)

Stuart, Madeline, 2020, *Madeline Stuart: diversity advocate and the world's first Down's Syndrome model*, Purcell, Emma, Disability Horizons. Available at https://disabilityhorizons.com/2020/03/madeline-stuart-we-speak-to-the-downs-syndrome-disabled-model-and-diversity-advocate/ (accessed 22 June 2020)

Stutzman, Matt, 2012, *Paralympic archer Matt Stutzman shows how to fire an arrow without arms*, Foreman, Glen, The Advertiser. Available at https://www.adelaidenow.com.au/sport/more-sports/paralympic-archer-matt-stutzman-shows-how-to-fire-an-arrow-without-arms/news-story/b090c44c7997ef7e4c3685230d8f849c (accessed 22 June 2020)

Thunberg, Greta, 2019, 'When haters go after your looks and differences, it means they have nowhere left to go. And then you know you're winning! I have Aspergers and that means I'm sometimes a bit different from the norm. And - given the right circumstances- being different is a superpower. #aspiepower' posted on Twitter, 31 Aug 2019. Available at https://twitter.com/gretathunberg/status/1167916177927991296?lang=en (accessed 22 June 2020)

Vujicic, Nick, 2010, *Life Without Limits*, Bantam Doubleday Dell Publishing Group

Zayid, Maysoon, 2014, *I got 99 problems... palsy is just one | Maysoon Zayid*, TED, 3 January 2014. Available at https://www.youtube.com/watch?v=buRLc2eWGPQ (accessed 22 June 2020)